SECRETS OF AN ISLAND GIRL

SECRETS OF AN ISLAND GIRL

HOW I LOST AND FOUND MY MIND IN PARADISE

Jean V Roberts

March 2015

ISBN: 1514610949
ISBN 13: 9781514610947

A Yellow Blouse

⁂

It's my 48th birthday, November 4, 2010. I am in the Oprah studio audience. Me. Little old Jean Roberts from the Golf Course road in Grand Anse, St Georges, Grenada.

Oprah walks onto the stage with her shoes in her hand. My breath is suspended. My heart is full. I can feel the tears coming. I am in the presence of the woman who changed my life. I am in the presence of the famous Ms. Oprah Winfrey.

I have dreamt of this moment. Well I have dreamt of a similar moment, one in which I am sitting on the stage with Oprah discussing my life story. Yes, it's been a dream of mine for as long as I can remember. But here I am, experiencing the next-best thing - sitting in her studio audience.

She has sat in my living room via the television set for the past twenty years, telling me I am good enough, brave enough and smart enough to live my best life. Day after day, I would sit in my Canadian living room at 5 p.m. and listen to her tell me I was talented enough. She suggested books for me to read and introduced me to the most influential people I have ever known. She said I needed to believe in myself.

For years, I have seen her as my sister, my friend, my confidant, my go-to person.

So I travelled from Banff, my home of fourteen years, with my friend to see the show. Unbeknownst to me, my women's group that meets every Tuesday had written a letter to the Oprah show announcing my arrival.

Dear Oprah,

Tomorrow, November 4th, 2010, you will have an exceptional woman sitting in your audience. She is travelling happily from Banff, Alberta, Canada to experience the actuality of a dream she has held to be on your show.

Jean Roberts moved to Canada a little more than two decades ago, from Grenada. She had been on a spiritual journey of sorts, taking wisdom from influential teachers such as Marianne Williamson, Eckhart Tolle and Wayne Dyer.

Recently, Jean has become part of a women's group (that's us) that meets every Tuesday to talk about life, joy, hope and love. Through the discussions that evolve, we also reaffirm wishes and experiences that we want to manifest.

That's where you come in, Oprah!

Jean's wish has been to come to your show for quite some time. Every Tuesday, it has been part of her affirmation. She admires and respects the woman that you are and how you have chosen to live your life. You have been with her throughout her journey.

So you can imagine the excitement when she received an email just two weeks ago, congratulating her in winning the lottery to be in your audience. It just so happens that November 4th is her birthday. Winning the tickets, on her birthday? Oh my god ! We are all believers in our dreams coming to life!! We are so happy for our friend, our sister to be living in the moment.

Having told this story to you, Oprah, what are we really asking you for? Well, being believers, we know we can ask for what we want and we can allow it. We would love for you to shake her hand after the show.

In closing, we invite you to take a moment to look at this link and you will see the essence of this wonderful, amazing woman.

Sincerely Yours
Leigha, Fern and Breanne

http//www.banffcraigandcanyon.com/articledisplay.
aspx archive=trueande=2806799

No, I did not get to shake her hand that day. I got to see her and be in her space. I felt her energy. After the show we went over to her store and I bought a yellow blouse with gold trim around the bottom, from Oprah's very own closet.

Two things happened to me the moment I saw Oprah. One: I recognized I was watching her do her job. The irony of that! I came all this way just to watch Oprah work. It struck me as funny. All these years I had watched the show, never once being aware that it was just a job she did very well. Yes, I can be naïve.

Two: I sensed her tiredness. It was her last season. To be really honest, I felt extremely disappointed. There I was, desperate to meet Oprah, wanting to tell her how much she had helped me in my life, wanting to worship at her feet, my feelings strong and overwhelming, but it was all I could do to keep myself from crying. I wanted to shout and run to the stage saying, "I love you!" In my mind's eye I could see security dragging me out of there, calling me a crazy woman and getting the police to lock me up in an asylum. All I could think as I watched her on stage was, "If I shout or make one wrong move, everyone here will know I'm crazy."

I was there watching Oprah, my idol. But in my mind I was in the fantasy I had had all my life. I sat in the audience, struggling with the reality crashing into my fantasy, holding onto myself for dear life. It was all a bit surreal. Something that I was not allowed to dream of came true. I never believed in a million years that I would be sitting in the Oprah show audience. It just had never crossed my mind as a real possibility.

I remember one day I was saying to a friend. "I can't believe the Oprah show is coming to an end! I wish I could see her before it's over."

My friend looked at me funny and said "Then why don't you check online for tickets to the show?"

That was it! That was all I had to do! It was that simple.

THE LITTLE
OLD HOUSE

❦❦

THESE ARE THE STORIES MY mother told me.

When I was a baby, no more than three or four months old, my mother would wake up in the dead of night to find me barely breathing. She would take me to her bosom and pray that I made it until the morning. Fighting to keep me alive, with fear and guilt in her heart, she would rise and pace the tiny room and hall board house she called home.

There was barely enough floor space for her to pace and the house was bare. Nothing hanging on the dark wooden walls. One single bed, the one she rose from, sat in a corner. The other kids slept on the floor, on old rags we called bedding. The other room had a table in one corner. Nothing else.

In her desperation to keep me breathing, she'd place her mouth over my nostril and suck the snot from my nose, tears running down her face and into her mouth, mixing with the snot. As soon as day broke, she would leave the house to take me to the doctor. For five miles, she'd walk and run up the hill along the narrow, uneven stone path that led to the gravel road and down the grassy golf pasture passing the greens and the sand pit, not noticing her surroundings in her haste. She walked through the cane fields, feeling small and vulnerable. The cane swallowed her, giving her a certain protection. Yet the leaves were swaying in the wind, looking like shadows of men coming at her with blades in their hands. She would arrive at the doctor's way too early and wait 'til he opened the office. Somehow she felt relief just by being there, felt like she had done her motherly duty to save me.

I was not a wanted child. Being in her early twenties and struggling to raise three fatherless children on her own, when my mother found out she was pregnant again, the thought of having another mouth to feed pushed her close to the edge. She was ashamed and overwhelmed. She did not want anyone to know for fear of being judged, so she had tried to hide her pregnancy.

In her despair and loneliness, feeling once again without a man to stand up with her, she had turned to the bush doctor - also known as the obeah woman or man - for help, and was given leaves of a special bush to abort the pregnancy. This did not work as well as she had hoped, but going to a modern doctor had been out of the question. She just could not afford such luxuries.

My mother was not a special case. Early abortion by drinking bush tea was a common practice on the island. It was our only birth control method. The only other alternative was to climb up the plum tree and jump off. She just did what most women did back then. In some cases, it worked and in others, it was too late. In my mother's case, it was too late. She had to carry the pregnancy to term.

Unhappiness settled in her womb. Nine months of carrying an unwanted child while working hard as a maid all day, then taking care of the three children she already had at night, hoping God would take care of this somehow, She is doing the work, but hoping someone else would arrive and take care of it all for her.

That's why my father came into her life.

My mother had met my father when he started renting the house next door by Tanty Violet, in the Stones. He was a pastor in some little church. At the time my mother was still Catholic. She said it was never a one-night-stand thing. She never brought him home because of the other children. She was still grieving her other childrens' father, who had ran off to England with another woman. But really, she had thought, "Finally, someone is here to save me and the children."

Alone, with no one to turn to, my mother felt her only option was to get rid of the baby growing inside of her. The bush tea did not work. The pastor did not want his congregation knowing about this, so he was not there to help.

With three mouths to feed and one more on the way, she felt broken and weary but had no choice but to do what she felt was nearly impossible.

My mother's mother gave away her four daughters. I call her my mother's mother because I never knew her the way a granddaughter knows her grandmother. The few times that I met her, I thought she was an interesting person. She'd walk barefoot and carry her shoes tied into a headscarf on top of her head. She died when I was about 12 years old.

She gave my mother to a distant well-to-do relative, who took her in. My mother was not alone there. Other people's children were also living with them. Some days they would send the children to school, and some days they would keep them at home to work the plantation. Back then when you lived with a family, your life consisted of three things: work, sleep and a good beating. Education came last. That was my mother's environment, growing up.

When she turned fifteen she left for the city and settled in Grand Anse. She was fortunate to get a job as a house-maid with a white Grenadian family. They had three kids, two boys and one girl. This family became her family. It was the kind of family my mother would have chosen, if she had had a choice. She gave them most of her love and her time. We got the leftovers. We got the tired, angry, resentful woman who had to come home and feed four mouths after being on her feet all day doing the same thing for someone else. She never took my hands, never gently stroked my hair to soothe me, never kissed me on the cheek. Instead, she would cup her hand to the back of my head to push me along. I never got her love, her hugs, her kisses. I never knew what it felt like to be held in her arms, never got to smell her scent. I grew up within this void of her absence, with the sense that I was raising myself. In a sense, my mother had raised herself, too. So, she did to us what was done to her.

By age five, I was left alone at home while my mother worked all day and my older siblings were at school. If ever my brothers and sister were around, they would leave me behind like bread crumbs.

I took to wandering around the neighbourhood sucking my thumb, which was the only thing that interested me. I sucked the big one on my right hand for 14 years. It was a source of comfort. Every so often my mother would go through certain phases where she would get fed up with my thumb-sucking and try something drastic to make me stop. Once she dipped my fingers in chicken shit. Another time, she spit on my fingers. This went on for years, but I continued sucking until my one-eyed uncle rubbed my fingers in his old kakajay eyes. He actually did this twice before I stopped. Soap and water were my good friends.

There was a narrow dirt pathway we used as a main road to and from our house. It ran right past the Nori's big house. Their dog would run down their concrete driveway and chase after anyone that went by.

One day as my brother and sister walked past the Nori's house with me trailing far behind them, the dog rushed out. They ran away and left me standing in the dog's path.

The dog bit me on the bum.

The Nori's drove me to the hospital in their fancy car. The big hospital sat on the edge of the rocks right above the sea. The windows were whitewashed and weather beaten. When we got there, we had to wait to see the doctor. I looked out the big window. It was like looking through the frame of a picture, a picture of the blue, blue yonder of turquoise water and clear skies. They gave me a tetanus shot right in the same place where the dog bit me, so I cried. The Nori's were so sweet. They held my hands, and when it was over, they got me hard pink and white candies, the ones that come without the wrapping paper.

Another incident happened on that same path where the dog bit me. We were heading to the pasture on that dirt road. It was the safe way to go. We could go from our house to the Golf Course pasture, and to all the neighbours' homes in our community without having to cross the main road. On this particular day, a young man about the same age as my oldest brother was cutting the bush in front of his house with a cutlass. He stopped for my siblings to pass, then continued cutting. He didn't even see me tagging along behind them. He hunched over the grass swinging the cutlass above his shoulders and sweeping forward to make contact with the bush. As he lifted the blade the point cut my head between my hairline and forehead leaving a gash about half of an inch that healed into a scar.

When I was seven years old, Grenada hosted Expo '69 and also had its first Circus show. The island was buzzing with excitement and anticipation. None of us kids could sleep. The streets were cleaned and many visitors arrived.

I was standing half-naked with my mother by the side of the main road, under the flamboyant tree known in the U.S. as the Royal Poinciana. The tree was like a landmark in town with its red and green flowers always in bloom. It was right at the base of the little hill where we lived. My mother was sweeping the ground under the tree.

Across the street, I could see our famous Grand Anse beach with lots of little fishing boats bobbing up and down in the water close to the shore and beyond that, a few big ocean liners, anchored out at sea and lined up along the horizon. We call it the imaginary line in the Caribbean Sea, that solid line where sea and sky meet. And as a kid I always wanted to go beyond that line. I wanted to know where the ships came from.

As I wondered how the ships so magically emerged from the sea and sky, a young pregnant woman came to talk to my mother.

The three-legged woman at the circus was freaky and spectacular. When it was time to see her, I covered my eyes with my hands, peeping through my spread fingers wanting to see her but at the same time not wanting to see.

A few days later the young pregnant girl moved in with us. We were living behind Ms. Philip's house at that time, in a two bedroom house made of boards. Our house had a living room plus two bedrooms and an inside kitchen, which was quite rare. The homes we lived in before had outside kitchens or no kitchen at all.

She was the first of a string of young women, some pregnant and some not, that came to live with us. My mother gave one room to the pregnant girl and the other she shared with us kids.

From that day on we had a parade of young homeless women living in our home. Brenda, who had a baby named Cathy. Mary, who slept with our cousin Tony. Hanna, Mary's sister who married Tony. Red Sandy from Saint John. Dark Sandy from somewhere in Grand Anse. And Sasha who saw imaginary men hiding in the corners of our house in the middle of the night.

Sasha would wake up at night, whimpering. She would sprinkle liquid from a bottle in each corner of the bedroom. Terrorized out of her mind that ligaroo were watching her (the Caribbean version of a vampire) she would ask, "Can you see him?" My sister and brothers and I would all huddle together in a corner, teeth-rattling scared, wondering what would happen to us. This went on for months. I heard my mother say, "Somebody do Shasha."

When Caribbean people say "do" like that, it is a code word for Obeah or Voodoo. And somebody do Shasha something. Nobody knew exactly what, but Sasha's behaviour was enough for people to say she was done.

I heard that sort of thing all the time as I was growing up. Obeah was in the air as an invisible source, like the wind blowing. We could not see it yet we knew it was there. We could feel it.

This was the language I grew up on. I had to be careful to not cross anyone or look at anyone the wrong way, for fear they would do me. I was scared shitless of Obeah. I did not truly believe in it, but I didn't have to. Obeah, Voodoo was woven into my cells like the threads that held my clothes together. It was the very culture I lived and breathed. It was lurking in every dark corner, and around every bend, and it was on everyone's mind.

Eventually my mother asked Sasha to leave, but the list of homeless women that lived with us went on and on. In today's world, my mother would be called a foster parent.

We moved a lot throughout my childhood. We stayed in similar little old houses, mostly houses which consisted of two rooms, a bedroom and a hall. The hall was used as the living room, kitchen and extra bedroom. We called those "room and hall" houses.

Our moves were all in the same neighbourhood. We moved from the Stones. Grenada has six parishes and each parish is made up of countless little villages with names like the Stones and Hungry Hill. Then we moved to the Golf Course, down Grand Anse Road, then back to the Golf Course then to Belmont then back to the Golf Course a couple more times before making it our home in the early Eighties.

At age thirteen or fourteen my mother sent me to live with my father's brother, Uncle John.

Uncle John, his wife, their three children, his mother-in-law and his nephew all lived in a big house in the back of the Golf Course, in an area called Woodland. The house was built on three levels. The main floor had a big kitchen with a real fridge and stove, a dining room, two bedrooms - one for the boys and one for the granny - a washroom, and even a utility room. The top floor had the master bedroom, the girls' bedrooms, and a private bathroom. The bottom level was a sunken living room with a big piano in one corner.

I moved in and became their live-in maid. I used to believe my mother had sold me into slavery. All I did was work hard for people who I thought were out to see me suffer.

My job was to do the household laundry. I would wash clothes by hand, standing over a tub and wash board. It took all day.

Each morning I also had to prepare school lunches for all of the children, which got me behind and left no time to shower or comb my hair. Aunty, Uncle John's wife, would tell me I was nasty. I did not know how to take care of myself.

Most Friday nights, Uncle John would take me and the two boys to his chicken farm in St John. We would leave home around midnight and drive for what seemed like hours in Uncle John's car. The car was so old, it would shimmy and shake on its wheels as we drove. Sitting inside the moving car felt like being physically shaken by someone. The roads to St. John were narrow with deep curves, making the trip nightmarish every time. By 3 a.m., we would be plucking the chickens to be sure they were ready by 6 a.m. for the Saturday morning market.

I was not sure why I was sent to live with my Uncle John. Maybe it had to do with my not learning much in school. My mother wanted me to have an education and to be looked after by people she thought could afford to do so. I understood now that my mother sent me there hoping I would have a better life. But nothing about living with my uncle and his family was better.

I had lots of chores to do. I never felt comfortable in my own skin. It seemed like the rules were different for me. I had no idea how to take care of myself. I couldn't do my own hair. I went to school every day with my hair in knots. The grandmother never helped me. She was too busy making me feel unwanted. I knew I was not liked, especially by the grandmother, who had been happy having a room to herself before I showed up and ruined her life. She would do small, cruel things like give her grandchildren snacks after school but not give me any.

One day, at school I went to the bathroom. Blood was all over my panties. I thought something evil was flowing from my vagina. I had sinned and was being punished, blood everywhere. It held me captive and paralyzed for a moment. I could not imagine what was going on. I told the teacher. She called my aunt to let her know and I was sent home.

When Aunty got home, I was sitting on the swing in the back yard, pushing myself back and forth, scared out of my mind, I didn't have a clue what was happening to me. She gave me some big maxi pads in a brown paper bag and told me if I let a boy touch me, I would have a baby. I believed that for sometime and would not go near any boys. At some point, it started to make no sense. I would get touched by boys yet no baby would come. I spent years confused with that and my mistrust for all adults only grew stronger.

I attended the Berean Christian Academy School with the other children at Uncle John's house. The school was formed by an American husband and wife missionary team. It was located in an old abandoned hotel called Island View Hotel.

The Hotel sat atop a hill right above the harbour with a panoramic view of the ocean. The main floor of the school was designed as an office space. Each student had their own cubby hole. Our desk had wooden panel walls on either side. We couldn't see the other kids, unless we stood up or pushed our chairs away from the desk.

Everything about the Academy was rich. Our uniform was a one-piece dress the colour of a bright green apple with a belt that tied around the back. We wore a white shirt underneath. The dress was modest and had to be worn below the knees. The kids were all from the rich neighbourhood, with parents who could afford to pay the tuition fee. My mother wanted the best for me, so she made a trade. I lived with Uncle and helped them out with the house work. In exchange, he paid my school fees.

The Berean Christian Academy school was supposedly all about Christianity. God was used as a verbal abuse tool. Everything I did seemed to fall under the "sinful" category.

I was accused of kicking a teacher. The teacher had pulled me up from my chair. My feet got caught in the leg of the chair and, as I yanked them loose in anger, one foot hit the teacher. I was suspended from school for being rude with an attitude.

Still, the Academy was not all bad. Lots of great things happened as well. Each morning before we sat at our cubicle, we would sing and pray. And I was a center on the school netball team.

We played lots of games with the other schools. We never won a single game and I didn't like losing, but it was fun on the court. The other girls would whip our butts and called us rich bitches. I played a mean game, running up and down the court, taking the ball from the other team and passing it to my team members.

I played a flute in the band. I wasn't great at that either, and I still can't play the flute or any musical instrument. I also sang in the choir. We lost a singing competition too, singing "Inch worm, inch worm."

Our study materials were custom-designed for the school. At the time, I didn't get why our workbooks were called "pace books" but since each student worked independently on their own book and at their own pace, now I see the reason.

The thing about studying like that was, some students got left behind. I was one of those students. I went from a poor, public primary school where everyone was studying at the same pace and moving to the next level together, to a rich private school where everyone studied independently. The odds where not in my favour. I was not set up to succeed.

The Grenada school system requires student to pass Common Entrance exams in order to go to high school. You can only take the Common Entrance exams twice. I took them both times, once while I was in the primary school system and once at the Academy, and failed both times. I couldn't continue in the Academy after age 16. By that age, if you hadn't passed the Common Entrance exams there was nowhere to go. So, I was out of school.

After being put out of school, I was sent back to my mother's. My mother, not knowing what to do with me, sent me to secretarial school.

The owner of the school was also the teacher. Her idea of teaching was to take her ruler and pound the knuckles of my hands with the sharp edge, every time I hit the wrong keys on the typewriter or came to school with long fingernails. I liked keeping them long. I failed secretarial school, too.

It seemed I would fail at everything.

BEACH LIFE

❦❦

"Miss Tourist......Miss Tourist!"

I turned around. My brother, Michael was across the street in his company van, grinning from ear to ear as he looked at me.

"Miss Tourist," he said again in a softer tone, "where are you going?"

I smiled back while lifting my shoulders and speaking with my hands. I did look like I had stepped off of one of the cruise ships that lined our harbour. I was wearing a flower print cotton halter dress, a wide-brim straw hat which framed my oval face, and thong dress slippers on my feet. My cocoa brown skin glistened with coconut oil. I was no more than a hundred pounds - slim, sexy and pretty but not very much aware of that.

That was my thing, getting dressed up to go to the beach or visit my friends. Usually I would meet my friend Liz on the beach. Liz loved the beach more than I did and I loved, *loved* the beach. Our daily ritual was going to the beach as soon as we woke up, staying until sunset, picking up beach tourists, then going home and getting dressed up to go out with our new friends. This was our life.

When I look back at that time in my life, it seems like one big beach party but I had many jobs. I cleaned and washed part-time for American Medical School students. I was also a housekeeper at the Cuban barracks, and a cook and waitress at the Italian restaurant.

In later years I would hear Oprah say a million times over that her grandmother, while hanging clothes on the line, had told her "Pay attention! You will have to do this someday!" Oprah said she had a knowing that was never going to happen. I could relate. Her story gave voice to how I was feeling back then. I knew in my heart I was no one's housemaid. Mind you, I have worked as a housemaid many times over.

I stayed at home with not much to do. We were living in Belmont at the time. Most days, I would get dressed and go down the road to the post office to hang out. We did not get much mail but I loved going to the post office. On my way, I would meet up with Lyn, Bobbi and some other friends. Lynn was tall and very thin with a broad mouth and wide nose yet she could pass as a super model. Everyone called her sexy. But Bobbi was the one I was closest to. She was my best friend. She was beautiful, with fair skin and long soft curly hair, and because of that combination, we called her "cullie." Her mother was black and her father was a Grenadian Indian man. We didn't go to the same school, but Lyn and Bobbi hadn't gotten into high school either. So we became friends on the road, on my daily walk to the post office. I had no close friends until I met these girls, and they were the first friends I had.

For a while we hung out every day on the street corner. We would get dressed up with nowhere to go. We were nicknamed the Donna Summerses of the island. We were innocent, naive and brave. We would hitch rides going nowhere. We would get into a car and get out once the driver reached his destination then turn around and do the same thing going the opposite way. My only worry was to make it back before my mother got home from work. The whip came out if she got there before I did.

One day I stopped my mother from beating on me. Our family was living on the Golf Course. I had come back from the sugarcane area, down the Golf Course pasture. My friends and I had been hanging out all day doing nothing but roaming the area, my favourite pastime. I would spend the whole day wandering around a new area, or walking the beach for hours at a time climbing the trees, looking for crabs or just moving, looking around, hanging out, discovering new things.

Whenever I didn't make it home before my mother, she would take out the whip, and the whip would be anything she got her hands on. That day she was sweeping the yard with a broom hand-made from a tree branch while chatting with a friend. As she spotted me coming, she went into her usual rage.

"Where have you been? Your friends are dragging you astray! I don't want you hanging with them!"

As I came closer she tried to grab me. I stepped back, standing my ground. Lifting myself up, I looked her in the eyes.

"You are never going to fucking hit me again," I told her. "This is your last try."

As soon as the words were out of my mouth I sprinted into the house. She came after me. I jumped out the back door.

I moved out that same day.

My friends and I rented an expensive villa on a quiet beach from an old rich man. Lyn said her father, who worked on a tourist ship, would pay the rent. The thing is, Lyn had a tendency to lie. Every time rent was due, we had to beg for money to pay.

One of our rich English neighbours, Owen, was a bachelor. He was black, smooth, and handsome with an English accent that could charm the pants off an old lady. Owen would help us with our rent for the price of walking his dog. He had two great big Dobermans. I was scared shitless of those dogs but I took them out every morning.

The villa had bougainvilleas lining the side of the house along the walkway and steps leading down to the beach. We didn't stay there for long. We could not sustain such a lifestyle.

We would spend the day on the beach, eating our meals from tourists and the local vendors and at night we would crawl through the back window of the villa to sleep. We did that for two months before the owner wised up to us and locked everything down.

I moved back home, pregnant.

My mother never laid her hands on me again.

I had gotten pregnant one hungry night while out scrounging for food. My friends and I were at the Golf house top apartment, at a late-night cookout party. I ate until my belly was full and was having a great time. Until I had to pee.

The bathroom was between the two bedrooms. To access it, you had to enter through one of the two bedrooms. I went through and was sitting on the toilet with my panties down around my ankles when Tom came into the bedroom and stood in the doorway with an evil grin on his face like a cat in the cannery. I finished peeing fast and grabbed my panties to pull them up, but he was faster, grabbing my biceps and pulling me into him. I begged him to stop, pushing him in an effort to get away but he threw me on the bed and jumped on top of me. I kept trying to get away, kept begging him to stop. He kept at it, telling me how much fun I would have.

Lyn came into the room. I screamed for her to help. She stepped out, laughing, powerless, saying, "I can't get involved."

Later she would tell me, "I thought you were fucking joking."

I was at a house full of people and no one came to my rescue. No one even knew I needed rescuing. "Rescuing from what?" they would all have said. "Tom is harmless!"

When he was done, I pulled myself together, acting like nothing had happened. I rejoined my friends.

A lifetime later, and I am still acting like nothing happened. Or so it seems.

That's how I got pregnant. Once I found out, I started climbing plum trees and jumping off in hopes I would lose the baby.

When my mother found out, her first question was, "Who is the father?"

When I told her who it was, she became enraged. She dropped what she was doing and went to give Tom a piece of her mind.

My mother stood by me like a rock through the entire pregnancy. She became the father, mother and grandmother - until the day she left for Canada, about two years later. My son Sam was born healthy, happy and beautiful. He is my only child.

Tom came around after Sam was about three months old and took him to see his grandmother who would identify her blood. She did this by looking at the baby's head, face, belly, hands and feet, turning him over and checking him out the same way a doctor would give a baby a check-up. The grandmother declared the baby was theirs and that was that. Tom became a father to the baby. His mother became a huge part of the baby's life.

Tom's mother would take Sam to her house regularly. She disregarded me from day one and never treated me with respect.

"What type of young women gets herself pregnant?" she said.

She herself was an upstanding citizen, a police sergeant, a wife and a mother of five boys at the time. Her two older sons, Sam's father and his older brother were both involved in the government. What they did with that power was unspeakable, but somehow it was me she blamed.

Being a mother did not stop my lifestyle. I lived the same way as before, going out and about whenever I wanted. Both grandmothers did not trust my skills as a parent. They wanted to do everything themselves with the help of my older sister and so I let them, because it was easier to go out than to listen to them judging me.

One day while hanging out with Penny outside the movie theatre, we met Bernard, a Swiss man, and his friends. Bernard owned a yacht. His two friends also had their own yacht. He invited us on board. We spent the next few days hanging out with Bernard and his friends.

I stayed on Bernard's yacht and Penny hung out with his other friends on their yacht. Penny was glamourous and a bit older than me. She had this dark, edgy beauty, with high cheek bones and skin the colour of cocoa, and a small straight nose with almond-shaped eyes. Her breasts were big, round, soft, and womanly. The rest of her body was slim and hard. She leaned slightly to one side when she walked, and stood with one hip higher than the other.

They never quite liked Penny because she asked them for money. Bernard asked me to sail with him to Venezuela. I said "yes!" but told him I was only going if Penny and my other girlfriend, Camela, could come too. It took some convincing, but the other boat men agreed.

We needed visas because Grenada was considered a revolutionary island and was seen as Communist. We received our visas within the week and before we knew what hit us, we were sailing away to Venezuela.

We headed for Los Testigos, a small cluster of Venezuelan islands. I was on Bernard's yacht. Penny and Carmela were on Bernard's friend Nan's yacht.

By the time we arrived in Los Testigos, trouble was brewing on Nan's yacht. Penny wanted Nan to pay her for sex, while Carmela was giving it away for free. After a few days on Los Testigos, a decision was made to take Penny and Carmela back to Grenada on Bernard's yacht while I stayed on in Los Testigos on Nan's yacht.

As soon as they set sail and left the bay area, the girls jumped overboard with their passports. They did not want to leave but there was no place for them to go but to get back onto the yacht.

The yacht ended up in Trinidad because of weather. At the time, the Trinidadian government wanted nothing to do with Grenada because of our revolution. All Grenadians had to have a visa for entry, which the girls didn't have. So Trinidadian Immigration would not allow the girls to get off the yacht.

The situation got worse when Carmela snuck onto the Island illegally.

The port authority seized and searched the yacht. Keeping them all in Trinidad for a few days. They took away the firearm on board and roughed the men up, then asked them to leave Trinidad. They would return to Los Testigos about five days later with Penny still on board but no clue as to what had happened to Carmela.

In the meantime, I was in my own paradise hell on Nan's yacht with his crew man. He spoke French, I spoke English. We were on a Spanish island. Not a good mix for communication especially when my friends were the cause of the trouble that was going on. The French crew man I was left with was very angry and he took it out on me. We got into our own fight. I can't remember what that damn fight was about. It had to do with being frustrated over communication, and hunger too, I believe. We started arguing, shoving each other. We wound up rolling around the deck on top of each other in a real fight. I held a knife to his face and told him he was a dead man. Our neighbouring yacht man, a friend of Bernard and Nan's, saw us fighting and came to my rescue. That was how I wound up staying on the beach and eating with the local fishermen and their families. I spent two nights on the beach sleeping in a local fishermen's hammock, totally in awe of the beauty of the island.

Once Bernard and Nan returned with Penny, things did not get any better on board. Penny had to stay on the yacht with me and Bernard. Nan wanted nothing to do with her. She tried to get Bernard to have sex with her but he wouldn't.

We stayed for a few days exploring the islands of Los Testigos, swimming in the beautiful tranquil waters, lying on the pure white sandy beach. Los Testigos was a tropical paradise, quite peaceful. Most days it was just us, the sea, the sky and the sand. On other days it was us, the sea, the sky, the sand and the fishermen out at sea.

Bernard loved diving. We would take the dingy out to sea and he would dive for lobsters. I would sit in the dinghy alone, waiting for him to emerge. He would stay under for long periods of time, diving with only a diving glass and snorkel.

Then we would have beautiful dinner parties on board with our lobster catch of the day.

One day, on one of the smaller islands, we went hunting. I did not know what we were hunting because they were using the French word for "donkey." We caught a big one, skinned it, and hung most of it to dry on board the yacht. Knowing it was donkey meat was a bit hard to digest, but I tried some.

After a few days of lazing around on the amazing Los Testigos, we headed to Margarita Island. We cruised into a marina packed with yachts, all kinds of them, varying in size. Another beautiful sight.

Los Testigos had been beautiful and tranquil but Margarita Island, that place was buzzing and alive. It was like a big party and everyone was invited. The Venezuelan women were beautiful. I had never seen such beautiful women in my life. They were colourful, with bright smiles and very sexy. I spent many hours admiring them.

Bernard and Nan wasted no time in getting a ticket for Penny. They got her on the first available flight from Margarita to Grenada. She wanted me to go with her but I didn't. I stayed with Bernard. He wanted me to stay so I did. Penny was really upset that I stayed. She told lies and spread rumours to everyone including my sister when she got home to Grenada, that we were being abused on the yacht and that's why she had returned. No one questioned her story. She had returned and I had not and Carmela was still somewhere in Trinidad, so there was no one to counter her lies.

Hanging out on the yacht in Margarita Island, now that was the life! Each night, we would have dinner on a different yacht. We made friends with all the yacht people. I spent hours people-watching from our yacht with binoculars, sometimes watching other people watching me. I would take showers on top of the yacht, naked while others watched. It is just what yacht people do.

Bernard would go off for hours at a time helping everyone with yacht issues. That was the kind of man he was. He would spend the day in the water underneath someone's boat doing repairs. I would get so upset with him sometimes for his generosity towards others but that's also what I liked about him. He was such a caring man, always kind, putting others before himself. He was older than me by about 20 years. He had been married and divorced and spent seven years building the yacht we lived on. His dream was to sail around the world and he wanted me to go with him.

We stayed on Margarita for some time, sightseeing, fixing the yacht and partying.

I experienced my first birthday party ever on board the yacht. It was my twenty-second birthday and I had never had a real party created just for me, with gifts and cake and punch. What a thoughtful and beautiful gift that was.

For the first time in my life, I felt loved, really loved. But I did not know what to do with such love. I got drunk, really drunk, the vomiting kind of drunk, at my own party. I had to be put to bed while the other people stayed and partied on my birthday.

Such a new experience for me. Bernard had just wanted to show me how much bigger life was outside of my tiny island of Grenada.

On that same day, before my birthday party, we had been hanging out in this beautiful house owned by the Adidas shoe people. The house sat on a hill with a killer island view. We smoked some pot and I tried the first and only snort of coke in my lifetime. I snorted only in one nostril which affected me in the same way a head cold does. It was just not my thing.

We left Margarita Island and sailed to Cumana on the mainland. We spent a few days in Cumana, made some new friends, and left the yacht in the marina. We took the bus to Caracas then another bus to Mérida, a famous area in Venezuela where the world's longest and highest cable car is located, on the snow-capped Andes Mountains. Bernard wanted to show me what snow was like.

"This place reminds me of Switzerland," he said.

The road to Mérida was the most dangerous mountain road I have ever been on. At each corner was a group of crosses representing the number of people who had died while travelling that road.

The elevation going up on the cable car was so high, I remember having trouble breathing. I got the flu just from the experience of being in the cold. My first snow experience was literally breathless. One moment I was down in the heat, a few minutes later I was high up in the mountain playing with snow, then back down to the heat.

We returned to Cumana to find our dinghy stolen. We stayed a few days, enjoying the activities on the beachfront, with vendors selling everything under the sun.

We finally sailed back to Grenada. The return took much longer as we were sailing against the wind and along the coastline. We stayed a few days in Grenada, long enough to spend some time with Sam. Then we sailed on to French Martinique, stopping on all the islands in between.

We arrived in Martinique in the middle of the night, a couple of weeks before Christmas. I woke up to hundreds of yachts in the bay. It was an amazingly beautiful sight.

French Martinique had a unique feel about it. The island was bright, vibrant, and full of colourful people. It did not have the sex appeal Margarita Island had.

For the yacht people, it was like France. They could get everything French there. All the supplies and parts for the yacht were easy to find on this island. Every single European yacht would stop there.

It took two minutes to walk into town from the yacht. Most days I would swim to the beach and hang out for a long time alone, people-watching and swimming. Bernard spent his days helping his fellow yacht men fix and clean the bottom of their boats. Bernard worked so much that we did little sightseeing. Everyone wanted his help and he had a hard time saying no. At night we would hang out together on each other's yachts.

I left Martinique along with Bernard a few days before Christmas.

I found out I was pregnant. Bernard wanted to marry me and take me around the world. All I could think was, "I haven't lived yet."

I flew back to Grenada on a little island plane. Days later I had an abortion.

Bernard came to Grenada about a month later, hoping I was still pregnant. He wanted to take me back to Martinique with him. He was deeply hurt and cried like a child when I told him I had aborted. I felt his pain. But I was twenty-two and already had a baby, whom I had left with my mother to go gallivanting all over the place. I was not mother material. He was twice my age and wanted desperately to father a child. I had no idea what my life had in store for me but I did know I was not ready to be anyone's wife.

Then the Italians arrived, three of them, to open a restaurant in Grenada. I met Franco the first year he came to scout the island for a suitable location. I hung out with him the whole week he was in Grenada and he paid for whatever I wanted and gave me money too, promising to give me a job when he and his partners returned to open the restaurant. And he did.

Franco was a bit of an eccentric man. He was afraid of almost everything but especially of dying. He was short but handsome, in a Danny Devito of kind way. He walked around with wads of cash on him all the time. He was generous. I liked him but I did not care for him as my boyfriend.

I got the job at the restaurant as promised and started hanging out with all the Italians. I had my eyes on the youngest of the men, Bruno. Bruno was a pretty boy. All the women wanted to fuck him. All of us wanted him, me, Penny, Liz, Penny's sister and every other women on the street. And I think we all did fuck him at some point. Bruno did not know which end was up with all the women offering their pussy to him. He was just not used to that.

Then one night I slept with Medico, the last of the bunch.

Everyone at the restaurant usually went out partying after work on the weekend. Sometimes we hung out at their place up in the hills. They lived in a beautiful house with views of the luscious green hills surrounded by grafted fruit trees, and bananas, and coconut trees. We would walk around the grounds naked, smoking pot and picking fruits from the trees with our hands. It was a private oasis. Adam and Eve come to my mind along with all the forbidding Christian stories.

One night after a party, I pretended I was drunk and lay down on the hood of the blue Volkswagen that Medico drove. He lifted me up and put me in the car and took me to their house along with the others. When it was time to go to sleep I climbed into bed with Medico.

That was the night I understood what passionate love making was. As he loved me, kissed me and fucked me, my body burned with the sensation of passion, underneath my skin and in my heart and a heat in my pussy that never stopped.

From that night on, Medico and I were an item. We were as tight as wax. That man loved me with the deep passion of his soul and I loved him back.

Penny and her sister Sue were upset with me again. It seemed like I was always getting in the way, blurring the line between money and prostitution. You see, Sue had made a fare with Medico when he just arrived and wanted him to pay her every time. But he did not like her at all and she did not want him either, until I had him. Now both Penny and her sister had a bone to pick with me.

The Italian Restaurant closed down about a year and a half later and Medico and the others went back to Italy.

It was my turn to be heartbroken and hurt. I threw myself into the only thing I knew how to do. I partied non-stop for months. I drowned my sorrows in the Grenada carnival, Carriacou carnival, and St. Vincent carnival, all in less than two months.

Home after a day at the beach

Always the tourist

My son and I

Yacht life

Doing Bad

I DID NOT BELIEVE IN the practice of Obeah. But I was afraid I would believe whatever the Obeah woman told me. I believed Obeah was real because of the stories I was told, the whispering lips covered by cupped hands telling of what was done to so-and-so. The religious shouting Shango people, and the Baptist people shouting till they fall beating on the ground like the hands beating the rhythm on a drum.

> *Obeah (sometimes spelled Obi, Obea or Obia) is a term used in the West Indies to refer to folk magic, sorcery, and religious practices derived from West African, and specifically Igbo origin. Obeah is similar to other African derived religions including palo, Voodoo, Santeria, rootwork, and most of all Hoodoo. Obeah is practised in Suriname, Jamaica, Trinidad and Tobago, Dominica, Guyana, Barbados, Grenada, Belize and other Caribbean countries.*

Obeah is associated with both benign and malignant magic, charms, luck and with mysticism in general. In some Caribbean nations, Obeah refers to folk religions of the African diaspora. In some cases, aspects of these folk religions have survived through synthesis with Christian symbolism and practise introduced by European colonials and slave owners. Casual observation may conclude that Christian symbolism is incorporated into Obeah worship, but in fact may represent clandestine worship and religious protest. [1]

Obeah was embroidered into the fabric of our culture. The environment was perfumed with it. Someone was always about to "do someone else bad." My friends would tell me, "Ah going and see how my light is burning" and they would go see the Obeah woman. I would hear this on the streets and in the neighbourhood. There was no secret to this. It was not hidden away like an American love affair, yet it was whispered behind closed doors. I believed Obeah to be evil, something to fear. I heard stories about the older Grenadian women, how their evil spells ruined the lives of others.

Penny's grandmother was one of those. She was feared by most. She would sit in the front doorway of her old house and watch the people pass by. She was in her nineties by then but we were still afraid of her. She was an old woman in a little old house that no one dared to visit. The

---

[1]   Wikipedia

braver kids would push their sticks into the space between the boards of her house and juke her with the sticks while calling her names. She was too old to cast a spell.

Back then, when a person got sick, they would first go see the Obeah woman to see what "do" them. No one trusted the real doctors. They never seemed to know what was wrong. When island people don't know what is wrong with them, which is often, they think, "The doctor still hasn't told me what is wrong with me simply because he just doesn't know." Many times people got sick and went to the hospital and just died without knowing why. Island people like to make their own diagnoses. So Obeah was big business.

Grenada's main Baptist religion was Shango. It was viewed as something to be feared. Our neighbour higher up the hill on the Golf Course was one of the leaders in the Shango religion.

Once or twice a year, she would have a two-week-long Shango dance ceremony in the front yard of her house, which was right next to the only main road on the hill. They would build a makeshift roof shelter that covered the entire yard space, in case it rained, and hang bright light bulbs in the ceiling.

Baptist Shango people came from all over the island and camped out for this shindig. They wore ritualistic head gear and white or red clothing. The daytime ceremonies were quiet but by later evening, the drums would start. Then you could hear the rhythm of the drums beating, matching the beat of your heart, seducing you like the hands of a lover. Your only choice was to come toward the beating of the drums.

Almost the whole neighbourhood would gather on the street in front of the house, watching as the Shango priests cut the heads off of young sheep and danced with the bodies around their necks as the blood ran down their skin. Some would drink the blood and smear it over their face. Others would run into the crowded streets with a cutlass in their hands. Some would writhe on the raw earth, beating around like worms. And as the drums got louder, the hands of the drummers invisibly fast, the dancing started. The dancers danced themselves into trances as they spoke in tongues that no one else could understand. They say they have got "the power." They are no longer themselves when in such a state, which makes them pretty dangerous. This would go on every night for two weeks 'til the break of dawn.

Watching them night after night is hypnotizing. You can't leave because you are afraid to go to sleep. The fear lay in the darkest shadow of my being, in the fabric of my life.

People were threatened by Obeah, too. Obeah was used as a threat on the island. It was seen as something worse than murder. Nothing good could come of it. It was used as a weapon to manipulate and control others. There are many stories about Obeah, but none can be proven in a court of law.

Whenever my friends went to see the Obeah woman. I would travel with them to Carriacou by the cargo boat.

Even though I went with them on many occasions, I never once went to see the Obeah woman myself. Instead, I would spend my time on the edge of the beach where the water breaks on the sand. I had my own belief about my life and I wanted it to stay that way. I did not believe in "doing bad." For my friends Obeah was their religion. For me, it was deep down inside like a root in the ground, unseen but part of the life of the tree.

One time my friend Lyn went to see the Obeah woman about a guy she was seeing. She wanted that guy to be more committed to her. The Obeah woman cast her a spell. Lyn did get a guy to be committed to her but not the guy she originally wanted. Soon after she had seen the Obeah woman, she moved in with this other guy, and he physically abused her. He would drag her out of parties and beat her all the way home. She was always battered and bruised liked a wounded animal. Lyn was a no-nonsense kind of girl. She did not put up with any shit from anyone. But this guy would give her a beating every week. I believed it was the Obeah woman's spell keeping her in that abusive relationship.

There are many similar stories and because of those stories I needed to believe only in good.

But in the wee hours of the morning, standing in the dark on the hill two houses down from my home, just above the peas tree in front of our neighbour's house, watching my friend's silhouette standing a few feet away from me, her face gleaming like black diamonds, something felt horribly wrong.

I could not run away from this. Going and seeing how to keep a man, and how to destroy the other woman was just a way of life. If you believed in it you were doing it.

I began experiencing unreasonable fears. One day, I would find myself no longer in control of my voice. Words would spill from my mouth like acid spilling onto an innocent bystander that got caught in a motor accident. This uncontrollable behaviour would go on for hours until I passed out and woke up in the mental ward of the general hospital.

But first I would live through another kind of crisis.

THE AMERICAN INVASION

I WOKE UP TO THE noise of the windows rattling, and the sound of my jar of hair grease falling from the dresser and hitting the floor. My comb and earrings followed.

The house swayed like a coconut tree in the wind. The sound of something heavy I had never heard before. A heavy engine. Everyone in the house was awake, asking what was going on. I thought is was an earthquake. But the sound was coming from above even though everything was shaking beneath us.

The sound keep getting louder and closer, everyone squeezed under the one bed in the house except me. I wanted to see what was coming, what the noise was. I peeked through the open window and saw the biggest plane I have ever seen, flying so low that the window cracked, causing me to jump into mid-air flinging my body to safety as the glass shattered onto the floor.

I ran outside and up to my friend Lyn's driveway and sat on the concrete wall fence. It was our favorite hangout with a wide view of the Grand Anse beach and the open ocean stretching out as far as the eyes could see. My adrenalin was pumping. I was in total disbelief of what was going on.

The Island had been on lockdown for the past six days, ever since a madman by the name of General Hudson Austin had come on the radio to say we were on a 24/7 shoot-on-sight curfew. Our beloved Prime Minister Maurice Bishop had been killed by his own political colleague.

Four years before the American invasion, Maurice Bishop, Bernard Coard and a group of liked-minded colleagues formed the New Jewel Movement Party. They took part in the 1976 Grenada election. They did not win. Three years later, the People's Revolutionary Army led by the New Jewel Movement staged a coup.

Eric Gairy, known as Uncle Gairy by his beloved supporters, became Premier of the Associate of Grenada from 1967 to 1974. Once Grenada achieved independence from Great Britain in 1974, Gairy became the First Prime Minister from 1974 to 1979.

He was a well-dressed politician, tall and dashingly handsome and extremely charismatic. He believed strongly in UFOs and at one point he wore only white clothing. Dressed immaculately from top to bottom, he loved to charm the Grenadian people, especially the women.

By 1979 he was seen as a dictator.

On March 13, while Gairy was out of the country, the New Jewel Movement Party led by Maurice Bishop overthrew the government of Eric Gairy, establishing the People's Revolutionary Government.

I was sixteen going on seventeen. What I remember about the People's Revolutionary Government is how upset my mother and most of the older people were. The island people loved Uncle Gairy and there was no way they wanted to back the New Revolution government.

All of that would change when Bishop, our new Prime Minister, started doing as he promised - promoting our agriculture, building the international airport, providing jobs and education for all. By the time the Americans invaded, Bishop had us eating out of the palm of his hand.

I became part of the young militia and worked as a first-aider. I would go on manoeuvres in the heart of the island, carrying an M16 with other young members of the militia. Being a teenager when I signed up, the chance to walk around with a gun was just too good to pass up.

I loved every minute of the short-lived adventure. We went out on weekends to different parts of the island. We would hike into the rainforest wearing camouflage gear with guns on our backs like real army fighters, and it *was* real for us.

As a medic, I learned how to bandage, give CPR, and carry wounded soldiers out of the forest. It was literally a fun time. Learning how to not only survive in the forest but also help my comrades was like reading a map of how to truly live a full life.

Bishop was a charismatic and visionary leader. When Bishop spoke at rallies you could hear a pin drop. Everyone listened. Nobody wanted to miss a word.

He was also easy on the eyes, as we say in the Caribbean, with beautiful light- brown skin. In his khakis, his uniform of choice, he reminded me of a movie star.

At the time of his death, Bishop was loved by many. He was murdered along with his pregnant girlfriend and many other supporters, by his political partner Bernard Coard because of some personal rivalry between them.

Bernard Coard put Prime Minister Bishop under house arrest, which triggered a huge demonstration. Students and workers from all over the island went to rescue their beloved Prime Minister. The demonstration spilled into downtown Saint George's with Bishop in tow, and proceeded to the fort where they thought he would be safe.

I heard about the demonstration at work. At the time, I was a housekeeper at the Cuban barracks. I got onto the back of a truck that was filling up with co-workers and we headed into town to take part in freeing Bishop. I got off the truck and moved through the crowd on my own as what seem like the whole nation sang: "We shall overcome, oh, deep in my heart I do believe, we shall overcome, some day."

We marched up towards the fort, while others gathered around the downtown market. The crowd was thick, the air filled with passion and freedom, everyone fighting for the same cause, freeing our beloved Prime Minister. No one suspected for a second they would open fire on us.

I was halfway up Kannas Hill towards the fort when the crowd came rushing down, screaming, some people covered in blood. Fighting had broken out between the Armed Force and civilians, causing many deaths. An armoured car came rolling by, firing machine guns at the crowd. I lay down in the gutter and did not move for what seem like an eternity.

The crowd was running and wailing above me while bullets flew over our heads. I felt I was going to die. I did not leave the gutter until the sky started to get dark and I knew night was coming. Then I made my way home on foot. I was worried. I knew that my mother and other family members had also been at the demonstration, but I hadn't seen them along the way. Everyone I passed on the street was asking if I had seen someone from their family. It was nightmarish, not knowing who was dead or who was alive, not knowing what the fuck was going on.

When I got to the Golf Course road a crowd was gathering to wait for news and looking for their family. We stayed up the entire night, with the island in darkness, with no news.

Finally, by the early hours of the morning, the madman Hudson Austin, part of the Bernard Coard's posse that had created the mess we were in, came on Radio

Free Grenada to say the Prime Minister Maurice Bishop was dead and the island was on a 24 hour shoot-on-site curfew.

Everything was on lockdown. We had no water, electricity or food. We couldn't leave our homes to find anything. Soldiers with guns patrolled the streets. Things got harder. We got hungrier. We were living under an unstable government and a lunatic that appointed himself leader. It was really clear that he and his people had not thought things through. They had no idea what to do next. We lived in this state for six days.

Then the American planes arrived.

Looking out that early morning, I could see the war ships lining the horizon. Men were literally falling out of the sky. Jumping out of the bombers with parachutes on. It was all so surreal. I was looking at a real live invasion. I was full of awe and amazement and yes, also excitement. Nothing seemed real any more. Little did I know, I was about to have my own invasion, of the mind.

The Americans came prepared to fight, and fight they did. What they did not prepare themselves for was how long the fighting would last. It took months. The island stayed under curfew for a long time, alternating between 24 hours shoot-on-sight, to nights only. The shops were closed. People did not work for a long while. The place was in pure chaos. The Americans fought against our men and killed the Cubans whom we all loved as our close friends. They were hard-working people who came to our homes to eat and party. They had girl friends and kids on the island, and some were married and making a home for themselves.

It was a shit show. We were a poor nation. We didn't have refrigerators. People usually went to the grocery store every day. Those of us who lived below the poverty line - that is, most of us - would beg our neighbours for food. We were all hungry.

Now we resorted to looting during the day. First we hit the big grocery store. The American soldiers left us alone. But then we started looting the School of Medicine, foreigners and rich people. That's when they would round us up at gunpoint. We stole food, clothes, jewels, anything that was not bolted down. This caused another type of war among the neighbours.

We lived in limbo, not knowing what would happen to us. Radio Free Grenada was down. We had no television. The only news we got was from the American soldiers fighting in the area. It was a scary time for all. We felt unstable, unsettled and shaken to the very core. People got mean, greedy and angry. Each one was in survival mode, every man for himself. All types of crime started happening after that.

The Americans thought they would capture Grenada within a few days. But the fighting went on from October 1983 to December 1983, between about 7,600 troops from the United States and the Caribbean.

By January of the following year the Governor General Paul Scoon was appointed leader of the island.

No one on the island was ever the same after the coup and the invasion.

The Revolution had been peaceful. We got a leader in Bishop, who had wanted the best for us. It was the first time that we as an island had had someone who cared what happened to us as a nation. Now that was over.

Before the invasion, Grenada had been just another island that nobody cared about. After the invasion, we took our place on the world map as The Island the Americans Invaded.

Today, when I'm asked where I am from and I say "Grenada," people just look at me with a blank expression. But if I add, "We were invaded by America and there is a Clint Eastwood movie to prove it," then their eyes light up with knowing.

IT ALL FALL DOWN

"Everybody! Everybody! Penny worked her obeah on me!" It must have been three o'clock in the morning. I was walking up the Golf Course Road, a road in a small neighbourhood of Grand Anse, with an actual golf course on the top flat plains of the hill. It is the only golf course on the island, making it quite busy in the tourist season. We lived on the second corner of the hill, on the road that leads to the actual golf course. The road to the golf course turns off from the main Grand Anse road, and leads up a very steep hill before flattening out into the open pasture that is our famous golf course.

Penny and I were on our way home from a party.

"What have you done to me?" I was screaming at her.

The first time I had met Penny was at the foot of the golf course hill. We were both dressed up, going out to party. It was around 1981, after the Grenadian Revolution but before the American invasion. I was hitch-hiking and so was she.

We weren't going to the same party. Penny had other plans.

She told me she was going down to the Barge, the boat where the Miami-based dredging company was doing excavation work, filling up the swamp down where the international airport was to be built.

I am not sure how Penny got hooked up with that bunch of men. But I am guessing it was pretty easy. The island is small and all the action happens in Grand Anse. Usually you only need to meet up with one person to know the whole crew.

Penny had invited me to go with her. I had seen her around before, but we ran in different circles. On this particular night when I met her, my life was about to change. But I didn't know it yet.

I wanted to be liked and Penny wanted me to hang out with her. We caught a ride to the barge and when we got there, a few men were hanging out on top. There was no party going on, just a few American guys hanging out. Call me naive, but I still did not realize that we were there to make a fare.

My new friend Penny told me to go with one of the guys and to ask him for one hundred USD. A hundred USD was a lot of money in 1981. I had not done this before, and I could not bring myself to ask for any money, but I did have sex with the American guy and he did give me money. I could not put a price on my body, but I was getting paid.

Did this act made me a prostitute? Yes, it did! I was sleeping with men for money. I couldn't see myself as a prostitute nor did I think of myself that way. At the time, I did not understand what a prostitute was.

After that first night on the Barge, Penny and I became fast friends. The Barge became a regular thing and Penny brought along other friends.

This was not a hard life-style. We did not stand on the street corner waiting to be picked up. I lived on a small island. I had no education and no job. I watched my mother work very hard and still struggle to make ends meet, having to raise five children on less than $200 per month. She would send us to her married boyfriend, to ask him for food and money. Mr. Wee, who lived with yet another women who was not his wife but he had children with.

Mr. Wee was a saga boy, a man who had land and money and knew how to win the local ladies' hearts, brown-skinned and what some would call handsome. He had a wicked smile that could melt your heart. He was rich by Grenadian standards. He owned lots of land behind the Golf Course where he grew sugar cane, corn, peas, potatoes and other local vegetables such as yams and dashine. He also had livestock. He would milk his cows and goats each morning and deliver the fresh milk. Mr. Wee owned a house on the hill where his children and their mother lived, and another house up Belmont Road about five minutes away where he lived with his wife.

He spent most of his time in his garden juppar. In this hand-made shack, he made barrels of bush rum. This was where my mother would send us weekly to pick up provisions and money. We got fresh milk from him daily for free. I am sure most of the women on the hill with fatherless children were also collecting milk from him daily for free. I must say, I drank lots of fresh cow's milk that curdled when you heated it on the stove. I don't think Mr. Wee ever learned to drive; he did everything on foot. He would walk up the hill almost every morning and down again at night. I really don't know how he kept all his women straight because I saw him going up and down the hill almost every day, delivering milk.

I could understand why my mother liked him. He was a kind and polite womanizer, which was accepted by the women on the island without question. As long as you could provide some money or food, the women would let you come around.

As children, we were the ones sent to ask the men for money or provisions, that is, locally-grown food. A lot of times, we would meet the men at the local rum shops. That was a regular thing we did as children. This was all around us. This was our life. Ask the men for money or provisions, and in exchange you got your mother's love.

My fares were nice gentlemen. I did not have sex with anyone I did not like or who did not like me. They were better lovers than the men I slept with for the sake of love. Through prostitution, I understood what it was like to have my body adored and not just fucked. I felt more love and affection from the foreign men than I ever did from my own Caribbean men, who just wanted to fuck and abuse me.

I had my first sexual experience, if you can call it that, at fifteen, with a guy in his thirties. I liked him a lot but he wasn't my boyfriend. I never really had a boyfriend to myself. Every guy I was with had a woman at home and a few on the side. This first one was a married man who just wanted to take advantage of a young girl.

He took me for a drive, then parked in a secluded area. I was protesting, I did not want to have sex there, but he pinned me down and fucked me on the wet grass on the hard ground as I fought to get away. I felt ripped apart in tiny little pieces, like my body was having an experience that my mind was not a part of. I felt brutalized, lying there on the ragged edge of the land overlooking the ocean. Beauty and brutality walking hand in hand. But I am getting ahead of the story.

So there we were, halfway up the hill from my house, just between Mrs. Ened & George's house on one side of the road, and Miss Eva's house on the opposite side. I could almost see Ened and George sitting at their window looking out to see what the noise was all about. They were always at that window, like fixtures looking out at everyone, minding everyone else's business. It was a daily pastime. It's what the older people did in those times.

I walked past Miss Eva's house and stopped above her garden. Her green peas tree was as tall as me.

I turned to Penny and said, "What have you done to me?"

I can't remember how the argument started. By then, Penny and I were so tight. Her house was two minutes away from mine. The interesting thing is, I don't even think I liked her. I never quite understood her greed and her two faces. She had this amazing boyfriend, an American medical student at Grenada's American medical university. He loved her, but still she made fares with every man she came across.

Penny's favourite pastime was seeing the Obeah woman. Penny was a seer, what we call a person who goes to the Obeah woman to see how her life is going.

At the time I knew no one who did good Obeah. I didn't think good Obeah existed in Grenada. It was all bad. We saw it as black magic. Penny visited the Obeah woman regularly the way you would go to church, even more regularly when things weren't going great. It was a family thing. Her whole family had a reputation of Obeah, of "doing bad." Her grandmother was a well-feared woman.

There were always conflicts between Penny and me. She was a greedy whore and I was a charitable one. I could not ask men for money but she demanded it. I was naive at the time. I couldn't understand why men preferred me over her. Well it could've been the fact that I was a charitable whore. But that's not quite true on its own. I was a gorgeous, sexy young woman who liked nice white men.

On that particular day, I was hanging out with Penny at her house. A few of us were there. She cooked a soup with dumplings and we ate.

We had a huge fight. She was sleeping with her sister's man for money. The sister found out her man was spending a lot of time at Penny's house and demanded to know why. Penny then told her sister I was the one sleeping with her man. One of our friends Sue and I were practically living at Penny's house, so it was easy for her sister to believe such shit. Penny's sister came into Penny's house screaming and grabbed me. We kicked and threw punches and pulled each other's hair. Well, I was so angry and pissed out of my mind and I let her have it. I was on top, winning the fight. A male friend, Mashy, had to pull me off of Penny's sister, who then went down to her house and came back with a cutlass. I had to stay in Penny's house until her sister cooled down.

I was seeing red. I could not believe Penny put me in such a position. But then, this was no exception. Shit like this happened all the time between Penny and me. There was the time I was seeing the Ambassador of Venezuela and Penny decided to sleep with him. When I got home after that fight, I remember walking into my mother's house and saying, "I think Penny 'do me,' I think she put something in the dumplin'."

I got dressed and went out to the nightly party, too pissed off to go with Penny. The thing is, we were hanging out in the same place with the same people so we ended up partying with the same group of men and got dropped off at the same time at the bottom of the hill.

It was hard being and not being her friend. This concept of being "done to" by Penny was always in the back of my mind.

I do remember how mad I was, and how much I believed that what I was saying at the time was true.

I was shouting and carrying on, nothing unusual for most island women. That's how we fight. We are loud and aggressive, shouting and carrying on for hours at a time. On this particular morning, I was fighting for my life. I wanted everyone to know I was in danger.

"Everybody! Everybody! Penny worked her obeah on me!" I was screaming at the top of my lungs and repeating those words. "If anything happens to me, she did it! She worked her obeah on me!"

On that fateful morning when I accused her of doing her Obeah on me, I believed it. I believed she had done something to get rid of me. I hadn't believed in Obeah or in doing bad until then, although I knew that people did believe and that it did exist. I guess I had made a choice not to believe in it. But there I was, in the witching hour of the morning, being burned at the stake, wrestling with demons, fighting the unknown. I was shouting, screaming at the top of my lungs, "Everybody! Everybody! Penny worked her obeah on me!" Was I delusional and making no sense? Or was that what was actually happening?

I felt my life was being threatened by some unseen force. I felt taken over by something mystical and surreal, indescribable. Words were spilling from my mouth like acid and I couldn't stop it, couldn't stop accusing my friend. I believed she wanted to kill me, wanted me out of the picture. I continued shouting out to everyone but no one in particular as if I were possessed, like I had gone mad. I couldn't tell you whether my friend was defending herself or not. I wasn't listening. The next thing I knew, morning had come and I was standing at the back door of my bedroom looking out at my neighbour's house, ignoring the stunning view of the ocean while still shouting and carrying on.

I don't think I stopped all day. My neighbours had turned into my enemies. My sister and her friends had become devils. My body was an island and my mind a revolution, an invasion and a tropical storm.

All of these came upon me in stages, unleashing their destruction for a period which would forever become known as The Year I Lost My Mind. It was the beginning and the end of my life.

THE UNIT

❧❧

I CANNOT REMEMBER GETTING TO the psychiatric ward. My sister later told me that she and one of our neighbours, Mrs Una, took me to the hospital where I was admitted to "The Unit."

This was after two days of non-stop shouting, cursing and ranting. I had packed up all my clothing, everything I owned. First I dragged them down the hill. Then I threw them in the garbage bin by the side of the road. My anger was deep, bottomless. I raged like a bull as I threw my belongings in the filthy garbage bin. My movements were that of a mad woman. I was flinging the clothes piece by piece into the bin, my beautiful aquamarine blue dress that I had paid a fortune for, my oversize neon orange sweater, a halter top, a bathing suit bottom. As each piece left my hands and entered the bin, I was saying things like, "I don't know who the fuck they think they are." I was saying this both to no one in particular, and to everyone.

After a short while, I took my clothes out of the filthy garbage bin and got on a bus and took them down to the Grand Anse Valley. I gave all my stuff to some girls I knew there.

Grand Anse Valley was a five-minute bus ride from where I lived. Most of the people who lived in that area were squatters. They had moved there at the end of Eric Gairy People's Government rule, before the Revolution. Apparently, even in my state of madness, I had had the sense to give my clothes away to the people I thought needed them the most.

Later I would find out that my sister had gone to the valley to collect my belongings. I am not sure what she said to get my stuff back from those poor people. She must have said something like, "Jean is not well. If she were, she would not give away her clothing." I can picture her anger as she says those words with a smouldering look on her face.

At the time I believed that the UNIT had once been the Doctors' residence. It was an old Victorian house with classic windows, hardwood floors, and high ceilings. Located on the left side of the General Hospital, it was on a private road where some of the well-off people lived with their million-dollar view of the ocean. The living room was open and spacious. We patients had a million-dollar view as well. We would spend many hours just watching the boats going in and out of the harbour.

Inside the living area were a small desk at the window overlooking the ocean and one wrought iron single bed beneath the window, close to the front door. The room was quiet with a gentle breeze coming in from the open window mixed with the scent of Dettol in the air.

I awoke on that bed.

I woke up from a dream that stayed with me forever. I dreamed I had slept for forty days and forty nights.

This dream was symbolic in two ways. The obvious one is that I must have been very tired and badly needed rest. That I believed with all my soul at the time, was all I needed. The other is the specific number in the dream: forty days. In the Bible, Moses was with God on the Mount for forty days and forty nights. The rain in "Noah's Ark" fell for forty days and forty nights. Jesus fasted for forty days and so it goes. Looking back, that dream was the beginning of my suffering. It was the premonition of what I would have to go through. It was also saying that my suffering was not permanent, that it would only last for a period of time. I often think of this dream and wonder what it meant. Partly I believed it to be a mystical experience, but I also believed it was my subconscious speaking to me.

As I lifted myself out of the deep dream, the first thing I saw was the nurse sitting at the desk at the window. She was very slim and fair in complexion, maybe in her fifties. She worked the day shift at the unit. She was kind and generous and showed compassion towards the patients. She took me for a walk once and as we walked along the road, she stopped to chat with one of the rich neighbours who was out front of her house with her big dogs. The dog circled around us, then bit me on the calves. It was the third time I had been bitten by a damned dog, but it was the first time it had happened in such a calm manner, without the drama of anyone running around making noise.

My initial stay at the UNIT lasted three days. Then I was told I would be okay and was sent home with some pills.

Taking the pills made me walk and talk like a robot with a funny expression on my face. My face was a mask of fear, twisted. When I looked in the mirror all I could see was a twisted, contorted image as if I were looking into a carnival mirror. I no longer looked like myself. I walked slowly and haltingly. My mouth was heavy and dry. I looked like an "imbecile," the word we used on the Island to describe a deaf and dumb person.

My friend Lisa came to walk with me up to the golf pasture. As we walked up the hill, passersby gave me strange looks. I did not catch on until someone crossed the street when they saw us coming. It had started. I was being treated like I had the plague.

I did not yet understand that things had changed, that my life had changed, meaning I was no longer one of them. I was now one of the insane. I had gotten something they were afraid would be contagious, something they did not understand, and the only way to keep it from happening to them was to treat me like garbage.

Yet apart from my robotic movement, I felt no different than I had before "the Incident." I continued to live the same life, as if nothing has happened. I had simply spent two days in the hospital.

I did not understand why the people I had lived among all my life were treating me like a stranger. They would tell me my mental illness was "good for me," that I deserved it. I had lived too much of a wild life, so it was good that this had put a stop to it.

The island is so small. Everyone knew I had been in the psychiatric hospital. The people in my community began to physically and verbally abuse me. There was nowhere to hide. I was taunted and teased every day.

"Crazy Jean," they would shout, "you old whore."

I developed a fear of going outside. It hit me like a tsunami wave smashing against the land, leaving destruction and debris behind, robbing the earth of its land. When this feeling of helplessness and fear came upon me, I would rush back the UNIT quivering like an animal out of its element.

The UNIT became a safe haven. The doctor would send me home again after a week or so, then I would return and the doctor would send me home again.This went on for a couple of months.

One time I left the UNIT stripped down to my panties and walked all the way home from town to Grand Anse along the main road. I wanted to show them what crazy looked like. News traveled fast. People came out to look at the crazy woman. The local buses full of passengers stopped to laugh and point at my nakedness. I learned recently that in some areas in Africa, when their sons are jailed unfairly, the women take off their clothes in public to shame the men and the people that put them behind bars. Maybe intuitively I was doing what my ancestors had done in the past, shaming the people who shamed me.

Since the unemployment rate was high, most of the men would hang out on the street corner from sun-up to sun-down. They littered the streets. Most days you would find them cooking on the street corners. That's a fact of life on an island as small as Grenada. The men's main focus was harassing young women on the street. They still treated me this way after "the Incident."

"Sweet thing, come here and give me some loving," they would call out to me. The thing is, it would always start out like they gave a fuck, but then, when I kept on walking, it was "Who the fuck do you think you are?" or "You're nothing but an old whore" or "Come on over and suck my dick. You're nothing but a cunt."

Now that everyone knew about my breakdown, there was a cruel sort of satisfaction to their taunting.

"You a crazy old whore. Now I can fuck you. Now nobody wants you."

I did not learn my lesson in all the many ways I was schooled on the roadside. I would scream back, cursing, using the same language as they were, letting them know they could not fuck me despite my crazy state. That would send them spitting in my face, slapping and shoving me round.

Over time, somewhere inside of myself, I started believing them. I would believe I was a good-for-nothing, crazy cunt. Then the tsunami wave of fear would hit me hard and send me reeling and running back to the UNIT.

One time, before "the Incident," I was in town with my friend Lisa around dusk. We got off the bus in downtown Saint Georges on the Carranage. We were on our way to the Italian restaurant to meet up with the owners. As we walked past the ghetto the hot limein, hanging out spot for the unemployed and drug dealers around town, someone shouted at me.

"Jean, you old whore!".

I looked over my right shoulder at them and said, "The trouble with you men is that no woman wants you."

German, a tall strapping red-faced guy with thick skin and the look of a wannabe gangsta and the same complexion as the singer/rapper Yellowman, crossed the street in a flash and slapped me in the face with the back of his right hand. The impact of the slap rocked me backwards. I screamed from the shock of it. He continued punching me in the head and face like a boxer. I crumpled to the pavement as my friend Lisa screamed and pleaded for help. The men on the opposite side of the street watched and did nothing to stop the brute from nearly killing me. As I lay broken and crumpled on the street, he grabbed for my friend but she started to run. He ran after her but she was quick and got to the steps of the restaurant before he could catch her. He returned and kicked me several times saying, "Take this!" and, "That's for your friend."

I lay there whimpering, feeling like the ocean had washed me up against jagged rocks.

Because I had been treated this way even before getting "crazy," I felt even more vulnerable and unsafe in my own skin.

So as I said, the UNIT became my refuge and stayed that way until the night I asked Nurse Harry for a glass of water.

Nurse Harry looked like a black version of a German SS officer, tall with strapping shoulders, but with a wide round bottom that seem to follow along behind her when she walked. Her face had the permanent expression of a vexed pig.

The night I asked her for water, she slapped me and said,"No."

So I went to the kitchen to get my own water. That made her furious. She grabbed the water from my hands and shoved me away. I fell to the floor like a cat on all fours. I crawled my way to the door then got up and ran towards the main hospital which was down a path from the UNIT and across the way.

The pregnant women hanging out on the balcony were the only ones up at this hour. When I got to them, one of them asked what had happened.

"She hit me!" I sobbed out.

By this time, Nurse Harry was coming to get me. They encouraged me to hit her back, and as she grabbed me, I hit her in the face. She dragged me back to the UNIT and stabbed me with a needle in my bottom a couple times.

The next day I couldn't sit down. The day nurse was appalled at what had happened. Nurse Harry did not get fired, but I got moved to the more long-term UNIT residence, which I nicknamed UNIT TWO.

My constant battle to this day is whether I am good enough, if am doing enough. I feel like a bottomless well that never gets filled up, and always have the need to do more, be more, work more, love more, live more, sleep more. Nothing I do is ever good enough. How can it be enough when the song in my head and the memory in my body is whispering, "Old whore, you're a good-for-nothing whore."

Fort Matthew Asylum

❀❀

I arrived at Fort Matthew, an old 18th Century fort that was used as the insane asylum, on a sunny evening in March of 1986. Fort Matthew had originally been constructed as the main barracks for the nearby Fort Frederick in the 1700s. Three years before my arrival, the Americans had bombed it after mistaking it for a barracks housing members of the local and Cubans militias.

This bombed-out shelter was now my residence. We women lived in a wooden structure on one side of the fort while the men lived on the opposite side in concrete barracks. In between us was a shell of a structure, hollowed walls with an underground passage and the old forgotten jail. To the right of the women's barracks were the Matron's offices, perched high above all the buildings with a view of the ocean. Everything around us look like the aftermath of a war.

The police had dropped me off naked, bruised and crying. I was put with the other women in the barracks. It was an open building with single iron-framed beds in rows, the kind you see in old war movies.

I slept through the first night, tired from my day of being beaten. The next day I was sent to see the doctor, a white American, an intern from the Grenada School of Medicine. He was appalled to see the blue-greenish bruises on my black skin.

"Who could have done such a thing?" he wondered out loud.

And in a quiet voice, as if speaking to myself, I whispered, "The police."

The day before entering the asylum, I was on the beach, still trying to live the same way I had before the breakdown. I did not yet understand that I had to change the way I lived. To get better, I would have to change the person I was.

I was cruising down the beach in my bikini. A few cruise ships were in our harbour and tourists took up most of the beach, all sprawled out and soaking up the sun. It was a beautiful sunny day with blue skies and the sun shimmering, glittering like diamonds on the aquamarine water. It was just another day in paradise, or so it seemed.

As I walked down towards the end of the beach past the Medical School towards Spice Island Inn, some of the male vendors on the beach - the usual suspects - started calling me names.

"Jean, you crazy old whore," one of them shouted.

Mirroring them, I shouted back, "Fuck you, mother cunt!"

Then one guy rushed towards me, putting his face close to mine as he shouted out the nasty things he would do to me, spitting in my face with each word leaving his mouth, threatening me with a beating.

This sort of thing had happened a lot. It was considered normal for some asshole to call me dirty names. The only difference this time was that now I was considered "crazy."

I turned away and continued walking as a cook from the Medical school restaurant, an older woman, called out to the guys to stop the cursing.

I stopped to chat with some of the foreign workers that were sprawled on the white and gleaming sand, catching a tan before going back onboard the ship to work. Mid-conversation, three policemen came up to where we were and gave me an ultimatum: get off the beach or get arrested.

"No," I said. I had no intention of either getting off the beach or getting arrested.

We exchanged some nasty words. All the while, the police were pulling me back and forth, trying to get me to go with them.

I knew my rights as a Grenadian. I had none. Guilty or innocent, when it came to the police, you were always wrong.

I was not disturbing the peace. I was simply talking with the tourists. The earlier fight was long over. But

Grenadian police were self-appointed criminals, criminals with badges. Everyone wants to be important, so they conferred importance on themselves. It is still the same way today.

So the officers started pulling me this way and that. I resisted arrest, fighting for my life, my rights and my humanity.

I put up a good fight, but three against one is not a fair fight. My bikini fell apart as they continued to beat me with their bootoo (what we call the baton). This went on right in front of the tourists.

They dragged me from the beach to the Grand Anse Police Station, about half a mile from the beach. It was too much trouble for them to lift me up and put me in a chair. I was dragged in and left on the floor. They handcuffed me to the leg of a desk. I was still fighting like an animal, wanting to be free.

"You are all criminals! You are all going to hell," I yelled.

And so I got another beating, this time by the policewoman behind the desk. She hit me with a piece of sugar cane, hit after hit, like a heavy rain fall pelting on a paved road. And all that time, I was sobbing, singing an old calypso song by Mighty Gypsy.

"Monday she went for cane, Tuesday she went back again, Wednesday must be gone for cane with man again."

She avoided hitting me in the face. I stopped singing. She stopped hitting me.

My body started to swell up. My head, back, shoulders and legs started turning purple. I peed on the floor of the station, there where I sat. By this time I was convinced: this is what crazy looked like. And if I were crazy, then any and all behaviour was explained away or accepted just by labelling it "crazy."

I was thrown into a cell for a few hours. Then they drove me - still naked - to town to see a doctor.

The office was on the second floor. We climbed the stairs and entered a bright, open space with windows overlooking the streets below and a view of the ocean.

One of the officers sat down on the chair in front of the big desk facing the doctor. The other one stood holding my forearm. My hands were cuffed behind my back and I stood there naked in front of the doctor, my head slightly bent in shame.

The officer in front of the doctor told him about me. I wasn't really listening. I was waiting for the doctor to talk to me directly. He never did. The doctor signed the document the police had brought. He did not even look directly at me, or ask my name. He just signed the paper. The police said I was crazy and the doctor agreed. In a sense, the police diagnosed me, not the doctor.

I felt powerless and alone. Despair hit me in a place beyond my soul, tears rolled down my cheeks, dripping onto my naked body. Even the doctor didn't give a fuck about me, I thought.

I was then driven up to Fort Matthew, the crazy house where patients lived behind high concrete walls with big iron gates, locked in.

Entering Fort Matthew reminded me of the song Hotel California: "You can check out any time you like but you can never leave."

After being examined by the foreign doctor at Fort Matthew made me feel better. Witnessing the disbelief in his eyes about the way I was treated made me feel cared for, so I held onto that kindness for a while. He had no power to remove me from the situation I was in, but he showed me kindness and treated me more like a human being than anyone had in the previous twenty-four hours.

But the truth was, I was in an insane asylum. I was in the real fucking CRAZY house, with other lunatics, therefore I was crazy too. I had no doubt in my mind. I had the proof I needed. I was in the asylum. I was crazy.

Most days on the inside were the same, except Sundays. On Sunday afternoons, the bus tours with island people would come to visit. They stayed behind the gates and viewed us like monkeys in a cage. The big wooden buses would park along the streets full of people dressed in their Sunday best, just coming from church, and other groups from various parts of the island.

The crazy house was one of the main attractions for the people on those Sunday tours. They visited all the institutions on the island: the prison, the asylum, the children's homes and the old folks' homes. They would bring food and clothing, so you would think they were being charitable.

I did not like those people at all. They would stand at the gate, looking very scared and excited to see the crazies and whispering, pointing, laughing at us. It is a weird experience to be looked at like that, as if you were a wild animal.

The other six days of the week, my daily living was the same. It consisted of hard labour, washing the clothes of the other patients over a tub and washboard, cleaning the rooms and making the beds, helping out with the meals and keeping the young pretty nurses company at night.

I don't know how long I stayed at the fort. Days looked the same as weeks. We would get up in the morning and go out into the yard. We stayed out in the yard all day, even on work days. We picked the leaves of the bushes in the yard to smoke as cigarettes.

Totan, a big black woman who resembled a big baby, would run around naked all day bawling, as if she were being beaten.

Iris, a skin-and-bone, hard-looking woman who was not afraid of hard work or a good fight was constantly making eyes at me. One night she crawled into my bed and tried to put her hands inside of my panties. I jumped out of my bed so fast and ran to the pretty night nurses. They treated what happened as a joke. I had a hard time sleeping after that night. The idea that a crazy woman - especially hard-ass ugly Iris - was going to crawl into my bed and try to finger me drove me nuts.

On any given day, I would daydream about my life. I would see myself going to the airport and getting on a plane, never looking back.

I had no idea how I had ended up in a place like this, and from the looks of things, there was no way of getting out. My belly churned with this knowledge. How did I get here? And how do I get out? I was trapped like a roach in a cupboard. What had happened to my life? Where was that girl called Miss Tourist?

For a while, I was a great patient. I did everything I was asked to do. But as time passed, wandering around the yard doing the same thing every day, not having anyone sane to talk to, started driving me crazy. I wanted out.

My reasoning was, if I am crazy, then I must do crazy things. But cleaning, washing and helping everyone were not crazy things. Spending my days in the yard of a bombed-out fort was not my idea of life.

So I climbed the cross.

Former Prime Minister Sir Eric Matthew Gairy had built a monument right next to the women's barracks at the Fort. The locals believed that Gairy had done this because of a belief in the supernatural and UFOs. It looked like a Christian cross with an array of lights attached. This cross, when lighted, could be seen from almost anywhere in St. George's and from the ocean surrounding the tip of the island. From a distance, the monument seemed to hover over

Fort Matthew. The cross was a tall wrought iron structure. I assumed Gairy had wanted to build something spiritual like the Christ the Redeemer statue in Brazil, something the people would remember him by.

There was only one thought in my head: "I am crazy." I could not get that single thought out of my head. "I am crazy" kept bouncing around the four corners of my skull.

"I am in a crazy house, so I must be crazy. A crazy person would climb the cross," I thought as I walked around the side of the women's shelter, stepped through the hole in the chicken wire fence, and walked towards Uncle Gairy's cross. I rested my hands on the metal beam, hoisted myself up and continued to move my hands to the next beam and the next beam, like I was climbing a ladder. I wanted to have a grand view of the island. I needed to do something besides sit around the yard with a bunch of crazy people smoking handmade "cigarettes."

I heard people shouting my name. I looked down from way up on the cross. The nurse was calling for me to come down.

"I am crazy, I am crazy, I am fucking crazy, and this is what crazy people do," I shouted back.

By this time I had a full audience under the cross, pleading with me to come down. I was so fucking pissed at the world.

How did I get here? How did I, Jean Roberts!! end up in the mental asylum? In the fucking crazy house with all these fucking crazy people? How the fuck did this happen?

Who holds the key to answering these questions? I know I have the keys but I can't find the fucking door.

I looked down from the cross, shouting at the wind, shouting at the people below.

"You all think I am crazy. What the fuck do you expect!"

I started a performance, a dramatic act. My crazy personality gave a bow and climbed down from the cross.

They immediately seized me for fear that I would try to escape. I was pushed to the ground on my back, hands in my face, hands on my head and neck. I was still struggling within myself, pleading silently to be let go, to be free.

The Matron came then. She was a fat woman with a round pretty face and trusting eyes. She wore a white traditional nurse's uniform with a white cap. She rarely left her post in the high office that overlooked all of St. George's and beyond.

The Matron gave orders to put me in seclusion. In a Fort built in 1779 as a defensive port, seclusion meant a concrete cell with four-inch thick walls and iron bars on the window, and damp, cold, mold-infested walls. In short it was no quiet retreat, that seclusion.

I begged and pleaded to be let out of that cell. I promised to behave. I cried for my mother, the only time I have ever cried for my mother in my entire life. I cried for my soul. I cried for the girl I would never again be. I was alone in the world. I cried myself to sleep in my new home, a real and ancient jail cell where war criminals were kept.

I knew how I had gotten into seclusion. I climbed the cross and declared craziness, and craziness gets locked down in old ancient cells, but I still didn't know how I got crazy to begin with. Did knowing that even matter anymore?

The morning nurse rattled the iron bars in the window of the thick cell door.

"Good morning," she beamed.

I asked her to let me out. "I can't until the Matron gives the orders."

She gave me breakfast and sat on the cold concrete surface opposite the cell along the long corridor to keep me company.

My cell was the last one down the long corridor next to the dark shower. After breakfast, I had to rinse the shit and pee from my cell, sweeping it all down the main drain that ran along the front of the cell. Then I was pushed under the cold shower. I was given clean clothes to put on, then put back into my cell.

This went on for a while. Time blurs or ceases to exist when you are sitting inside of a cell with no one but yourself for days. To pass the time, I would write on the walls with my dried feces, drawing things I can't remember, talking to children I didn't have. When the sun shone through bars of the high window on the back wall of the cell, I would watch particles drifting in the light. I would call them my children and sit and talk with them.

After days of crying and asking for my mother and asking to be let out, after nights of sleeping curled into a ball on the damp cold concrete floor in my daytime dress, I finally surrendered to the cold and the lack of human contact. I surrendered to everything that was not there. I was alone. Alone in a concrete tomb. Alone in the world.

In my world, the world that I created for myself.

I changed in that cell. I know this now. My acceptance of being in the world alone, my sad sorrowful self. I saved myself in that cell. I learned self-reliance, although I was not aware of that then. I was alone, but I had me.

I hunched over myself with sorrow and anger. I swore vengeance on all who took part in my being in that cold damp dark concrete tomb that served as a cell. This was the 80s, the disco area, for fuck's sake! Neon was in demand and young women like me were braiding, weaving, and wearing wigs. It was my coming-of-age time. It was supposed to be my time to exhale.

I got a neighbour in the cell two doors down, a thin tall dark guy with curly hair. He was very talkative and spent the day talking and calling to me through the iron bars in the door. He was a mild distraction. He represented life. I was not as alone as I thought. He blabbed on and on all day.

One night he fell asleep with a cigarette and set himself on fire. His blood-curdling screams and second-degree burns convinced the warden to let me out of my concrete tomb, saying, "It's not safe."

I came out quiet, quiet, my sorrow too deep, my anger too large to speak. I did as I was told. I no longer fought outwardly. Fear of what others can do made me quiet. The sweet trustworthy warden had locked me up in an old fucking cell and left me in there with no toilet, sheet, blanket, mattress or water. I had been left in a cold, damp concrete tomb. I couldn't trust anyone. Everyone in a position of authority - the doctor, police, my mother and the warden - had all proven unworthy of trust.

Not long after I came out of the cell, we were all moved to our new home.

Fort Matthew Asylum

Cell Block

Inside Cell

THE PINK HOUSE

✤✤

WE MOVED FROM FORT MATTHEW mental asylum in 1986, not long after I came out of the seclusion cell. It had been three years since the Americans had mistakenly bombed the Fort.

The contrast between Fort Matthew and the pink house was as wide and as deep as the ocean between the island and Australia. The fort was an old historical broken-down building with a life that had already been lived.

The name given to the new asylum was Mount Gay Mental Hospital, the same name as the island's famous rum. The pink house got its nickname from the vibrant pink paint splashed on the walls.

The pink house was like a neon sign. Everything about the pink house was new, the grass, the walkway, the gate. At Fort Mathew, the gate was very close to the women's shelter, so you could be seen sitting in the yard by everyone that came to the gate, including the tourists.

At the pink house, the women's lodge was a long ways away. There was more space to hang around than just by the gates. The main building had an entire floor dedicated to recreation and rehabilitation, which the fort did not have. The fort was dark and dreary, like a dungeon, an old castle falling down, broken and ready to be put to rest.

It was easy getting from the fort to the pink house. They just loaded us onto a bus. When we arrived, we opened the small gate and walked on the new concrete walkway towards our new home.

It smelled like a Grenadian Christmas morning. My family celebrates Christmas by buying everything new for the house. Instead of buying gifts for each other, my mother would buy new curtains, new cushion covers for the couch, new sheets and linoleum for the floors. The windows got washed and the walls painted, which made the house smell like a new doll. I have never owned a doll, but that's the smell it conjures in my mind. The scent of a new doll.

Everything at the pink house smelled new. A new day had dawned.

When we walked around the yard, we could see that the space was vastly different. For one thing, we had no view of the ocean. At the fort, we were so high up we had a view of the prison, and right below in the valley was the city, then the vast open ocean, which made the fort a vibrant bustling place. The pink house was secluded, tucked away in a corner on its own land across the river from the main road, in an area around St. Georges called River Road. You had to look for the pink house, but when you did, you couldn't miss it. It was so pink nestled amongst the natural green of the landscape, sitting there waiting for you.

The administration building was at the front by the gates. A long walk took you up to the main building, which had two floors.

The kitchen was a detached building at the back. Towards the right, behind the administration building, was the men's quarters and a little ways to the top was the women's.

The busloads of people no longer stared at us like we were caged. The buses still came but we were no longer hanging out by the gates. At this facility, the gates were guarded by real security men, which was both good and bad. They kept unwanted people out but they also kept us in and most days their only job was to shoo us back from the gates.

Being at the pink house was like living in a commune. The patients walked around muttering to themselves or talking out loud to the universe.

Nurse Harry from the Unit was now the head night nurse at the pink house. Imagine my surprise and terror when she showed up the first night, her big frame towering over us all. This time, however, there were lots of shiny new nurses on duty as well, so Nurse Harry's only crime was locking me up each night in the new secluded room, mainly because she did not want to be disturbed.

The patients at the hospital were all the same patients as at Fort Matthew. They lived there. It was their home. Sometimes someone would be sent to their real home but would return in a matter of days either because their own family didn't want them around, or because coping with people on the outside was terrifying.

Most of the things we did at the pink house were not very different from at the fort. I had my daily chores, bending over the tub, washing, than hanging the clothes to dry, watching the weather in case it rained. But it was my new beginning, a new place to start.

I behaved differently. Instinctively I knew I no longer belonged. Intuitively I knew I was not going to stay. My life was changing again.

I watched the young medical students who came to do their case studies. I wanted to be like them, and like the new shiny nurses who arrived. I wanted to be new, like the grounds and the building.

I would daydream of walking the beach and swimming in the ocean. I would dream about the life I would have if I were to become a nurse, walking on the outside without being harassed or insulted.

I would dream about taking the plane and leaving the island, going to faraway places, to countries I had never been to. I dreamt of a life that I did not think was possible.

The pink house brought new beginnings and new plans. The doctors wanted the patients to go home and not return.

The truth is, almost everyone who had been there is still there.

I don't know exactly why I left. But this time, I never returned.

It could be that I had learned the lesson to be humble. It could be that my life needed new direction. It could be that my life before the "incident" had been going nowhere and I got interrupted. Maybe I got to an intersection. Maybe I had angels who knew I did not belong in the institution. Or it could be the simple fact that I stopped fighting. I stopped fighting myself and the people around me. I stopped believing I was crazy. I never had been, or maybe I was for a moment. It is possible I was just tired and I needed to rest so I had a crisis. My mind did not leave me, it did not play any tricks on me. It could be my karma. But I believe I had a spiritual experience that led me to leave. It was a clear sign that my life was not going in the direction it needed to go.

The "realization" happened at an intersection. I had to choose between what I was told or what I knew. I chose what I knew. I chose me. I stopped mirroring the people in my community. I took the responsibility to look after myself. That freed me.

I started respecting my elders, the doctors and the young nurses.

Every once in a long while we would get someone new.

We got one new girl. She was as smooth and black as midnight. I had never seen anyone that black before. She was beautiful, like a black china doll. Her sadness floated around her like a winter coat. Her parents brought her from England and left her with us. We all wanted to play with her.

She spent her days singing to her parents who had gone back to England. She sang this song, a haunting sad song that she had made up herself.

"Stay with me mother, stay with me papa, can't you hear I am calling you, stay with me mother."

In the middle of the yard, on the way to the female quarters, were some old concrete staircases leading to nowhere, the remnants of an old house. I'm not sure why the builders left them there, but they served as a place to hang out. That is where the black English girl spent most of her time singing. That spot seemed to bring her comfort.

I also spent my free time sitting on the stairs, looking at the faraway houses in the surrounding neighbourhood.

I would spend hours in the kitchen with the cooks during the early part of the day, and late evenings were spent with the young nurses.

I began to forget what my old life was like. Time kept moving. Days passed into weeks.

I was unofficially counselled by all the pretty nurses in their crisp and clean starchy uniforms. They were new and young and in training and not yet strung out by the crazies.

We could tell the different ranks of the nurses by the colour of the uniform they were wearing. The dark blue uniforms with the white cuffed sleeves were practising nurses and the white uniforms were the head nurses. I loved the lilac uniformed nurses who chatted with me all the time. I saw myself in those young nurses. I often wondered how I had missed out on being one of them.

I remembered having taken an interest in nursing before the craziness but I did not have the prerequisite, a high school diploma, so I couldn't qualify. My education at the time was a grade 6 level. I had been told I couldn't learn, that I was stupid. There is this old calypso song that goes, "Schooldays were happy, happy days." It never made sense to me. My school days were nothing but beatings, which happened every day. They were just part of the curriculum.

I had lots of time to think about my school days. My memory of school was filled with straps, straps that would hit me over and over again in the palms of my hands and my wrists as well. Straps that would open my flesh. This happened most days, and when it was over and I got home, my mother would beat me for getting beaten at school. And so it went. The school straps were made from beach chairs, the thick plastic straps that are used to make the seat of the beach lounging chairs. So that was my daily dose of "school." If I did five mathematical problems and got two wrong, I got the strap.

It was like that in every subject because I had the same teacher all year. He taught all the subjects. Mister McIntyre was a tall, handsome man with beautiful lips, and oh how he loved the strap. That beach chair plastic strap was an extension of his very long arms. That's the educational world I grew up in.

Learning did not come easy. I could not learn in that environment. So I spent the first thirty years of my life in the illiterate, uneducated, ignorant community. Mind you, I did not see myself as stupid. I just did not know my capabilities. I still don't fully understand the things I am capable of doing. So, no, I never became a nurse.

Young nurses in Grenada were worshipped by the men. They were looked upon like they were somebody. All the men wanted a nurse as their girlfriend. In Grenadian society, being a nurse meant you were respected, you could sit up front, close to the bus driver. But being a nurse did not mean you were exempt from verbal or physical abuse. That was a given. It was part of the nature of the island people. Making others feel like they are nothing is in our blood. You don't have to take my word for it. Just ask any island woman if they have even been verbally or physically abused.

So there I am, in the loony bin, with the sense and knowing that I could be a nurse. I, too, wanted to be somebody. And those young pretty lilac-uniformed nurses treated me like I was a normal girl. They said I was different from the other patients.

They let me help them braid the others' hair. I used to help them a lot with Totan, the big baby. She ran around all day without any clothes on, sometimes crying just like a baby, only in an adult voice. No matter how many times you put a dress on Totan, she would rip it off and walk around naked. No one ever came to see her. I don't know if she even had family. Most patients were like Totan that way. They had no visitors. No one came to see them.

The environment at the pink house was less stressful. We were no longer in an old bombed-out Fort. My life had tranquility and more of a routine.

The pink house represented a new beginning, a new start. Looking back I can see my motivation to get out of the pink house had to do with the nurses in the lilac uniforms. Their pretty shiny faces and the idea that I could be one of them is what eventually kept me out of the mental asylum for good.

I was discharged six weeks after our arrival, and I never returned.

The shift between the old and new was a bus ride. That shift was the same as the shift inside of me. The old fort was a historical place where men were to be ready for battle, walking the grounds, maybe scared. Fighting amongst each other, pacing the ground, preoccupied with thoughts of getting back to their family, their lives.

The shift between living in an old space, where old voices and old energy were in the walls and permeated the environment with what used to be, and moving to the new the pink house where the land had been cultivated, new like a virgin, the soil was tilled, new ground was broken, new buildings put up.

There was no demon, no one that had walked the grounds before we arrived.

No energy living in the walls or voice whispering in the wind.

It was a new seed in the ground, new soil. All it needed was watering to blossom.

At the pink house, I was given my cocktail of pills when I got up in the morning, but my dosage was not as heavy as before. It was not the same as what I started with at the Unit, and it made a big difference in how I felt. I was not walking around the grounds like a robot, which was how I was when I left the Unit.

Doctor Dick, my very first doctor, had had no fucking clue as to what was wrong with me or how to help me, so he just gave me a very heavy dose of medication. My physical appearance changed.

We would have breakfast in the spacious dining room, not sitting on the ground in the yard in a corner to eat, as we did at the fort.

After breakfast, we got showers. I showered and dressed myself, and we would gather at the front of the male dorm where the nurses had an informal station. They would braid our hair and talk about their home life, things that happened outside the fence.

Then, it was on to my chores. As the day progressed, most of the afternoon was spent sitting on the concrete steps that led nowhere, with my new black friend singing her song. The truth is, her song was my song. Her life was my life. My mother was not there for me and my father was just a sperm donor. I was an orphan.

The sky was always so blue and the sun warm sometimes extremely hot the smell of the grass always present. The night sky was for the taking. My daydreams were the same: walking on the beach, free.

My rehabilitation was different from what the others received, because the young medical doctors could not find anything wrong with me.

I was not delusional. I knew what day it was and who I was. I knew who my family was. And I knew the queen was not my mother.

I was as normal as anyone could be.

I was capable of carrying out a task. My mind did not wander, unless I wanted it to. I was polite. I knew my place when questioned.

The pink house was a time to breathe in everything new. It showed me that I had a new life I needed to live. If I behaved normally. If I stopped cursing people and stopped going out at night to party when I was released from the pink house. I literally had to stop being the Jean I had always known.

The day that I left, I promised I was not coming back. I didn't make this promise to the doctors or nurses. I made the promise to myself. I needed to be a good girl. I wanted out of the asylum and off of the island. To get out, to leave, I had to prove to everyone that I could behave.

And although I did not believe that I had changed once I did get out, when I went to the beach, this time I understood that I was alone. No one would rescue me. Only I could save me. I had to rely on myself. I had to want to save *myself* badly enough.

Now, when I was shown just the slightest kindness and humanity, I recognized it within me.

When everything I had gotten was taken away, I was all that was left. Only Jean could save Jean.

I spent more time at home sitting on the steps. I went to the beach but it was nothing like before. I was waiting to leave. I cannot say what would happen if I did not leave because that was not the case. Every fibre of my being told me I was leaving the country.

Sure enough, one day my sister told me I was leaving. She handed me a ticket, a passport and a flight number. All I had to do was to get past Immigration and Customs.

THE SHIFT

THREE EXPERIENCES HAPPENED THAT MOVED me from mirroring the community belief that I was crazy to being more stable and grounded within myself. The experiences did not happen at the same time, but I can see the links between them and the awareness of the shift within myself.

The first thing that made me aware I wasn't crazy was being locked up in the cell. While in the concrete cell alone with my thoughts I had a knowing this was not my life. I had to get out of there sane. Although I was labelled a crazy person, nothing about me was crazy and deep down where it mattered, I knew this fact.

I did not have more than my share of madness - everyone has a bit of madness in them. I realized that what others were willing to do to me, like locking me up in a cold damp lonely tomb and making decisions for me without my input, was a bit mad. I had experienced what not having control of my own life felt like.

I surrendered to what I could not change. I also surrendered to the part of myself I knew had control over what *could* change. Reacting and acting out what crazy was is what got me in the mental asylum in the first place.

Locked up, I had been faced with sorrow, silence and nothing more to lose. I guess this is what AA calls "hitting rock bottom." This was my rock bottom. I had no place to go from where I sat in my cold damp cell. Everything was lost.

They say I lost my mind, and when I say "they," I mean everyone - the neighbours, the police, the people on the street. And while the doctors did not know what to make of my craziness, I found my sanity by myself, while sitting in purgatory. I found it at the edge of the cliff looking into my soul, knowing that silence was golden. In silence, I could hear my heart beating and my soul chanting "OM".

I sat in that cell night after night, alone with the voice of reason, *my* voice. It told me stories. It told me the only person I truly had was me and only me. I thought about the life I had before the asylum. I used to lie down at night outside on my friend's concrete fence, looking up at the night sky, counting the shooting stars and wishing upon them as they flew by. It was my favourite thing to do. Those memories kept me sane and strengthened my mind. I had dreamt of a better life while looking up at the stars and I knew I could do the same in my cell.

The other thing that made a difference was a young white American doctor at the Pink House. He was actually the second foreign doctor who showed me some compassion. The first one had been up at Fort Mathew. What he did wasn't like counselling. It was more like being seen, being treated with humanity and being heard. I realized how trampled on by everyone I had been, how looked down upon. I felt I was nobody. But this doctor talked to that place within me that knew I was good. He encouraged me to look after myself. He told me I could get better if I stopped listening to what the people on the street were saying to me. He told me I *was* different, and all I had to do was to stop coming back into the asylum.

With this new asylum, they wanted things to be different. So they started bringing in medical students from the Grenada School of Medicine to rehabilitate the patients.

One medical student wrote on his blog in 2005, "All of Grenada's 'chronically psychologically ill' are housed here. However, the lack of funding has turned it into more of a revolving door situation." The truth is, it has always been a revolving door. You would think that by 2005, things would have changed. But they have not.

I was a special case. I did not belong. No one, least of all me, understood what I was doing in there. I was not running around babbling. I had no delusion of who I or who anyone else was. I took clear directions and did as I was told.

From time to time, I would go down to the matron's office and talk with the nice white doctor. I was given lower dosages of medication and the doctor told me to rest when

I got home and stop going out at night. This doctor showed me respect. He treated me with loving kindness. He made me want to do better. He inspired me to look after myself. Just a little kindness can heal any broken heart. Just a little kindness can last a lifetime. That's how my healing started. It wasn't so much the healing of my mind as much as it was healing from the abusiveness of my community.

The third thing that happened to me sliced through me the deepest, hurt me the longest. It stayed with me forever.

One hot sunny day, after being out of the asylum for some weeks, I was standing on the big boulder in the front yard of our house at the golf course. The boulder was right beside the main golf course road which was no more than 25 feet from our house. I liked hanging out up on the boulder because I could see all the cars coming up and going down the hill. I could see them from our front balcony and from inside the house as well. That's how close we were to the road.

That day, I spotted a car coming up the hill. I recognized my son's father's brother as he turned the corner. My friend Bobbi was sitting in the front seat. I could see her clearly as the car came closer. Bobbi knew my house as if it were her own. She practically lived with us before going to England for a few months. While she was in England, I ended up in the "crazy house."

Bobbi and I had spent most of our time together. At 20, she was still very innocent. She liked to dig the crap out of her nose and roll it around her top lip as she sucked her thumb.

Bobbi did not have much. She used to sleep and wake at my house, wear my clothes, including my panties. She even wore my mom's and sister's panties. Her skin underneath her clothes was as itchy as mine was at the time. She had a shy smile and lovely lips. That is why the Englishman, well the Grenadian-Englishman, named Tom took her to England with him.

Tom was a dashingly handsome man. Everything about him was hot! His smile, his eyes, his kisses. He came to Grenada every year on vacation and would woo all us gals into hanging with him. We would live at his vacation home and he would feed and clothe us and give us money. He knew how easy it was to manipulate Caribbean women. He loved us all but he fell for her mix of beauty and innocence.

I knew she had returned from England but I hadn't gone to see her. I was sort of waiting for her to come see me. So when I saw her in the car from on top of the boulder that day, I thought she was coming to see me. I felt excitement and tears of joy.

But the car did not stop. Bobbi did not look at me. The car drove on almost in slow motion. There I was, standing with a full heart of expectation, happy to see my friend, to embrace her, to feel her love and friendship, but the car rolled on without her even turning to give me a second glance or smile of recognition. I felt like a nonperson to the two people in that car. I turned to stone, merging with the boulder I was standing on. I did not move. I waited in disbelief for her to turn around, to see me, but there was nowhere to hide from the truth. I was in plain view, exposed, yet invisible.

I can tell you this has to do with the mentality of the islanders. Somehow she had found out I was crazy and that was that. She could not come to see a crazy woman. End of story. I waited for her then and in a sense, I am still waiting. I haven't seen her since that day, not even once. That was twenty-four years ago.

The moment she passed me by changed my life forever. Everything I knew or believed was no longer true. I believed Bobbi was my friend but as the car drove past, that statement became untrue. Everyone believed I was crazy but that wasn't true either.

Betrayal was running through me like the blood in my veins. My world totally collapsed, crumbled at my feet. The smile on my face froze. Nothing, not the beatings by the police, not the ill treatment by my neighbours, not sitting in the cold damp cell, nothing sliced as deep as my best friend passing me on the street as though I were a stranger.

I moved slowly as though I were coming out of a deep, dense, fog and squinting as my eyes adjusted to the light of clarity. The kind of hurt that passed through my heart at that moment, the pain of betrayal, killed that old self in me. I knew I was done with that life. I heard a voice say, "I am done fucking around. I am no longer crazy. It's over. I am done with being a joke to everyone."

Have I ever forgiven Bobbi for abandoning me on that boulder, our favourite boulder?

All I can say is, "I'll show them."

VOYAGE

※

I LEAVE THE TERMINAL BUILDING and walk the twenty feet toward the plane. I start walking up the stairs feeling fear, almost paralyzed by it. I hesitate, wondering if I should turn around and look back. Should I turn and look at the blue sky, the green grass, the cows grazing in the nearby field, the people waving from the open balcony of the airport terminal?

I can't believe my luck. I can't believe no one has grabbed me from behind and started dragging me back to the insane asylum.

How is it possible that they have let me get this far, I wonder. Why haven't the police arrested me for false pretence? What's going on? I hold onto my sanity like a mother holds on to her first newborn, secretly afraid someone is going to snatch it away from her. The steps ahead of me look steep and narrow. My feet in mid-air feel heavy. Am I going to make it before they come for me?

All of this is swirling around in my fragile mind as I think back to the time when the airport was my refuge.

During my time going in and out of the Unit, I would visit the airport often. Sometimes I would take my kid Sam with me, stating we were leaving the island, but I had no destination in mind. I would take the local bus down to the airport and sit inside and watch the people come and go. I never tried to leave or get onto a plane but I would go to the counter and let the service people know that I was leaving the country. I would stay for hours until they asked me to leave. Then I would protest that I was waiting for my flight, which would cause a fight. Then the police would come and drag me back off to the Unit.

I never quite learned my lesson. I would go back again and again. I must have gone to the airport three or four times. And each time the police would drag me back to the Unit.

The airport represented transition, change. And being there was temporary. No one stayed there. It was in constant motion. People were coming and going, they were happy and sad, but feeling fully alive. It was a place where people showed their true emotions. When you arrive at the airport about to take flight you don't realize it, but you are no longer in control: Customs, airport agents and the pilot are in control.

I bring myself back into the present moment. I must have been moving. I am at the entrance of the plane. I turn quickly to take a last look around. As I do I make a declaration: "I am never coming back to this god-forsaken island. Never ever!!"

I make a gesture of throwing a stone behind my back. It's an old superstition, a symbolic gesture meaning, "no more, never again."

The air hostess greets me with a smile and points me to my seat. I know this is all real but I don't trust any of it. Getting on the plane, being shown to my seat, yes, it is real alright, but I'm afraid of being found out. Any minute now, they will know I am a fraud, an imposter. The police will be here soon, I am sure of it.

I sit and wait looking out the window. People wave from the terminal balcony. They have big smiles, some crying. I lift my eyes to the blue skies and green surroundings, the little colourful houses clustered on the nearby hills. I can feel the ease returning to my body, the excitement of the unknown and the chance to do it over, to have a life in which I waste no time and start to dream a new dream for myself.

I arrived in Canada on a beautiful September evening in 1988. The weather was slightly cooler than it was in the Caribbean. I stepped off the plane onto a long narrow covered walkway that took me inside the airport. It was my first time getting off a plane without seeing blue sky and feeling warm air caressing me in the face as it does when you step off the plane on any Caribbean island.

I arrived with one suitcase and some dreams: to get an education, stay healthy and write my life story.

I got through Immigration without a problem. My mother was there waiting to pick me up. She worked as a live-in nanny and was unable to take me in with her, so I was going to stay with my cousin Jane.

We drove from the airport to the east side of Toronto. My cousin lived on Coxwell Street. As we drove along the highway my eyes fixed on the sight of Toronto in awe of it all. It was so different from Grenada. I couldn't stop looking around. I had never seen anything like it.

Everything was massive. Huge buildings dominated the skyline. I was used to seeing the ocean everywhere. Now, it was building after building, reflecting the evening sun.

When we got to my cousin's place, she was happy to see me but it was obvious she was uncomfortable having me stay with them. I thought it was because my cousin, her husband and two children were all living in a one bedroom basement suite in a rooming house. I was told I could not stay for long.

At the end of the first week. I woke up to her husband kicking her across the floor. Then I understood the real reason she was uncomfortable having me around. Her husband beat her regularly but she did not want anyone to know this. She was afraid he would leave her if someone find out and called the authorities.

My mother found another place for me to live, with a woman she knew. She paid the woman weekly rent for me to stay with her. This did not last for more than two weeks either. This woman did not like me cooking with her pots and pans.

I left and moved into an attic room with two other friends. I gave them money to rent the room but they did not add me to the rental agreement so I had to hide each time I left or came home. The owner lived downstairs and was very strict about who lived in his place. Eventually, he found out and evicted us.

I moved back to the Coxwell area. This time, I rented my own room in a rooming house. I shared a kitchen and washroom with four African tenants.

At first I got jobs through a temporary agency, working in factories like The Bay and Toys-R-Us. Then I started working as a nanny, and I did that for a number of years. Every family I worked for treated me as one of the family. I was encouraged to take care of my health. They showed me that I too could have a better life, an education, and even dental care. I learned so much from each of them.

I was in the country illegally for five years, but for all those years I worked and took care of myself. I never once asked the government for help. I was told by many of my Caribbean friends and family that I should apply for refugee status, but I was not a refugee. I came from a Caribbean island, and yes, we had had a revolution, but the island was stable. At that time I watched my cousin Jane and many others apply for refugee status and collect welfare for many years. It was an easy short-term action to take. I did not follow the pack. I never did! Many of the people that had refugee status were found to have made fraudulent claims and were eventually deported.

I worked and tried to fulfil my dream of going back to school. I went to night school part-time in the winter months. My excitement of living in Canada keep me warm for many winters. I took a few classes in English, Math and Typing. My spelling was so bad that typing was nearly impossible to do. I could not learn. Taking night classes in Math and English was not enough. Night classes started with grade nine. I was way behind.

I liked being a nanny but I desperately needed something more challenging. I decided to work for myself instead. I started my own cleaning business. I started out by printing some business cards and putting a small ad in the local newspaper. I would go to the middle-income neighbourhoods and put my card in the mail boxes and knock on the doors and let the homeowners know what I was doing.

I got lots of cleaning jobs. I took the bus to all my jobs. I used the homeowners' own products to clean. I did not know what an overhead cost was, or anything about business. I would clean four houses per week and give discounts to the seniors. I was self-employed and made double the money I made as a nanny, plus had more time for myself.

One day I got a call from a business woman that owned a collection agency with her husband. She had gotten my business card from one of her employees that lived on the other end of the city. It took three buses and a train to get to her office. During the interview she told me she was impressed that I had gone out and marketed myself the way I did. She also asked me get liability insurance.

When she called to offer me the job, I told her I was illegal and I could not take the job because I was not insured. But she hired me anyway.

She said I had shown huge potential by putting myself out there. I got the job cleaning the collection agency's office at night and she also hired me to work as her full-time nanny for her newly-adopted baby. When I hired my friend to help me with the night cleaning, I became an employer. I had the best job with the best people.

Working for Jan was an eye-opener. I learned so much just listening to her. I believed she was my greatest mentor and teacher. Jan told me a lots about herself. She told me how she had failed her driver's test five times, and the reason why she drove such a small convertible car was that she was afraid to drive anything bigger. Because of that story, I never gave up when I took my driving test even though I failed four times. She had overcome lots in her life and her stories were my lessons.

Jan said I was her client and she was my client. I was not her nanny or cleaning lady. She made it clear that we were equals and treated me like a client and a great friend every day.

Her story inspired me to go back to school full-time. When I told them I was leaving to go to school, her husband told me all I needed to do was read the newspaper if I wanted an education.

Finally I decided the only way I could be free was to be a legal immigrant in Canada. I applied for legal status against all odds. Everyone tried to discourage me from doing so. My mother thought it was best for me to marry an African immigrant.

First I went to see a legal aid lawyer who told me the immigration law was changing and that I needed to apply under the Humanitarian Act and send in my form before January of the following year. I had no idea what the Humanitarian Act was but I thought the lawyer knew what he was talking about. That was the only advice I got.

I then walked into the Immigration office and asked for a form which I filled out and sent in. The next day I applied to go to high school full-time. When asked for my landing papers I told them that my papers were with Immigration. What I did not tell them was that I had only applied the day before, and that my chances of being a Canadian were very slim seeing that I had stayed in the country illegally for so long and Immigration was deporting Caribbean people by the planeload.

It took one interview with Immigration and a year-and-a-half wait to get my landing papers.

That interview was another life-changing moment. Up until then I was convinced I would be deported for staying in the country illegally for so many years.

The things I had thought would hurt me, like working illegally, running my own business and going to school were the things that saved me many times over. You see, almost everyone else I knew - my African friends and other Caribbeans - were all under refugee status and had refugee lawyers or they were getting married to someone with legal papers, most likely paying the person for marriage.

I would never forget the Immigration Officer who gave me the interview and rubber-stamped me to stay in the country. She was of Indian descent and that was surprising to me. I was so naive at the time. I thought only white Canadians were allowed to be Immigration agents. I also believed the whole immigration system was one person making the decision, like they do on the island. I did not realize that it took only one person in the system to decide your fate.

I showed up alone at the Immigration office in downtown Toronto for my interview. I was nervous and felt very much alone. When they called my name, I felt the fear rise in my throat. I wondered how I would answer the questions if I could not speak.

The officer asked lots of questions but the determining factor was that I had not been relying on the Canadian welfare system. The fact that I did all the things the law said I couldn't do like work or study were the very things that got me my landing papers in this country. My fearlessness in not following the pack or the norm is what got me my Canadian citizenship.

That was such a huge lesson. At the time I did not believe I would get my Canadian papers but I believed in the importance of having them. I knew despite my naïveté that the only way to really get ahead was to have my papers. And this stranger, the Immigration Officer, believed in my dream. We cried together when I told her the dream I had for myself. I have never seen her again, yet she was a big part of my life. I told her I would write a book about my life and I have struggled to keep that promise for twenty-five years. It is true there are people you meet for a moment that can change your life forever.

So I started school again at age 32, in grade 6, with extra credit for being an adult. Two years later, I received a senior English award at graduation and was accepted to college.

The two years I attended high school were the best, yet the hardest. I loved school. I loved everything about it. Well, maybe not everything! Taking exams was always challenging.

But going to school as an adult showed me I was not dumb or stupid as I'd been told. I was indeed capable of learning.

However, going to school as an adult meant I had to work to support myself. For a few months, I worked all night as a 1-800 phone sex agent. I quit because it was exhausting to work all night and stay alert in school all day. The school helped with bus tickets and free lunch but there were times I would walk the hour and a half it took to get there. There was nothing easy about being a mature student but it was so much fun to learn and recognize my passion for life, and for myself.

High school changed my life also in the sense that I understood my worth for the first time. It came in the form of a book. I read A Woman's Worth by Marianne Williamson and it change the very DNA in my body. Marianne mentioned in her book that she too had been in a mental hospital. She did not give many details about it but wow, did it hit me that intelligent people also get breakdowns.

High school was my saving grace. I got to see teachers in a different light. No one abused me. Everyone told me how well I was doing. I fell in love with everyone and everything again and again. I saw the possibilities in myself and I knew it was up to me to excel.

Four years later, I had a college diploma and a career in hotel management.

EPILOGUE

❧❧

TODAY I LIVE IN THE Rocky Mountains, in Banff, Canada's leading national park.

I am no longer in hotels. I am following the path of my inner vision that tells me I am here to help women, to show them the possibility of getting back up time and time again because the truth is, we are ultimately alone. My greatest lesson in life was knowing no one was coming to rescue me. I had to rescue myself.

For years I have told no one my story. I kept this secret for dear life, guarding my mind like a prisoner, feeling that if one person had an inkling that I had been crazy, locked up in a cell, my mind would just crack open and break. I thought I had lost my mind and therefore I couldn't let anyone know my secret. How could I ever say to anyone, "I lost my mind once"?

Meanwhile, my life was happening. I was working, schooling, buying properties, running a business, managing hundreds of people.

Finally, after years of bearing the weight of this secret, I went to an ashram for four months. An ashram is a spiritual place where people of all religions can go on retreat, rest or study. I did nothing but strip myself bare to get to know what was underneath every single layer and cell of my skin. I dug deep into my soul, mind and body, uprooting the layers and layers of crap that I was told by everyone. I got to see myself and understood that I had suffered; I had had a hard, rough and unspeakable time. And although that shaped me in a way, it did not take away the essence of what I am, my spirit, my strength. Having a fighting spirit is what life is about. I did not lose the part of me that knew who I was and what I was.

So here I am, 27 years later, living in beautiful amazing Canadian Rockies where the mountains are like my backbone and the surrounding nature is like my soul. This is where I live and this is how I live - in beauty, with beauty in my heart and soul.

After the ashram, I came to realize all I really could do was tell my story as I have always wanted to, to put it out there, to strip myself bare and say, "This thing has happened to me. It is not who I am, but it has happened to me. And it must have happened to other people in all forms of society."

I needed to share this with others. I want to say, "It is okay, *you* are *okay*." I want to share my story so you will know that no matter what happens in life, you too can live up to your full potential. My life is a map for living up to your full potential. When I look at how rough life was at twenty-four, how bleak and dark and without ambition and how low I was at the time, and then look at my life now, well, I would never have believed I would be living this amazing, beautiful rich life.

We do have choices. We can make it if we want to! We can be proactive in our life. We are gifted to begin with. This is why I wanted to offload my shame, rest it down and say, "Hey, look at me, I'm Jean!" I want to say this mostly to myself and the people of Grenada and the young women that are being bounced around. I want to say to them and to my young self, "You've got a life to live baby! You've got stuff to do and it is never, ever too late. Never, ever give up on yourself."

From the odyssey of my early life, I have learned that my mother wanted the best for me. She did not know how to give me the best but she wanted the best for me.

I learned from Uncle John that to be rich, I had to live poor. I had to work hard and eat like the locals. He had material things no other black person I knew on the island had, like a car, refrigerator, a nice big house, a swing in the backyard, a piano in the living room, an indoor kitchen and bathroom with flushing toilets. My uncle showed me another way to live besides being poor.

The Berean Christian Academy taught me I, too, could be part of a different life, a different environment. It gave me strength and showed me a different side of being rich that was really important.

My foreign lovers taught me how to love. What love could be, what love looked like. They also showed me another way of living very rich, not having to struggle or suffer for anything, a way of freedom. Yes, living on the yacht and hanging with the Italians was freedom. Freedom is a reality and it exists.

The invasion showed me that even a country could fall down. Things fall down and people fall apart.

I learned that Obeah, voodoo is just the other side of good and evil. It's like looking at the future with nothing to fear, but fear is part of living.

The friend who betrayed me taught me there are greedy people, and we all live in our own world.

I learned from sitting in a cell. It brought me to a place in my soul, took me to the depths of nothing and made me understand that life, when we quiet down enough, comes to nothing. We are ultimately alone. I was - and am - alone.

My friend Bobbi and the community taught me that we fear the unknown without questioning it.

I learned that leaving a place can bring a fresh start. And that change is good. It brings new chances to start over. Gandhi was correct. We need to *be* the change we want to see in the world.

Above all, I learned I can be free no matter where I physically live. Humans are more resilient than we are willing to accept. We are strong and we persevere. LIFE truly is a state of mind. Take Nelson Mandela as an example, he spent 27 years in prison and still became the President of South Africa when he got out. All because of his state of mind.

49601793R00077

Made in the USA
Charleston, SC
28 November 2015